Principles of Management

Principles of Management

C. Swarnalatha Raju
Assistant Professor
Department of Management Studies
K.L.N. College of Engineering
Pottapalayam

Publishing for future

SCITECH PUBLICATIONS (INDIA) PVT. LTD

www.scitechpublications.com

SCITECH PUBLICATIONS (INDIA) PVT. LTD.,
Plot No: 52, D.No: 2/619,
First Main Road, VGN Nagar,
Iyyappanthangal, Chennai - 600 056.
E-mail: scitech@airtelmail.in
visit us at : www.scitechpublications.com

Regd. Office: 7/3c, Madley Road,
T. Nagar, Chennai - 600 017.

Branches:

Hyderabad: scitech_hyd@yahoo.co.in

Kolkata: scitech_kol@yahoo.co.in

978 81 8371 629 1

Published by V. Ramesh for Scitech Publications (India) Pvt. Ltd., Plot No: 52, D.No: 2/619, First Main Road, VGN Nagar, Iyyappanthangal, Chennai - 600 056.

Foreword

The author of this book is an experienced teacher. She has used all her experience in writing this book. The subject is presented in a systematic manner and can be easily understood by the students. This book is primarily meant for the **B.E., MBA, B.B.A., and B.Com students.**

The book meets the requirement of the students and the teachers alike. I hope the students will be benefited immensely.

I congratulate Mrs.C.Swarnalatha Raju for this endeavour.

Dr.U.Suriya Rao,
Professor and Head
Department of Management studies
Madurai Kamaraj University
Madurai.

Preface

I am pleased to place this book in the hands of honourable academic community. Customer satisfaction has become a concern of highest priority. The primary purpose of this book is to prepare students to become successful managers. The material has been presented in a simple, clear, unambiguous and structured manner so as to engage the reader towards an appreciation of managerial responsibilities and challenges.

While preparing this book I have been guided by the requirements of the students to whom I taught this paper over the past several years. The students of Management & Engineering may become businessmen and industrialist. They must possess the requisite knowledge to manage the business effectively. I am sure, as they read the book, their doubts shall be removed and knowledge multiplies.

I express my gratitude to M/s. Scitech Publications (India) Pvt. Ltd., for publishing this book in a good shape and in short span of time.

I invite suggestions and constructive criticism from esteemed colleagues and promise to incorporate the same in the next edition.

January 2007
Madurai.

C. Swarnalatha Raju

Acknowlegement

I bow my head and thank **ALMIGHTY JESUS CHRIST** for having helped me to complete this book and his blessings has helped me to fulfill this endeavour successfully. I place this humble piece of work at his feet.

This **"extensive and exhaustive"** treatment of the area of Management would not have been possible without the moral support of **Dr. U.Surya Rao**, Professor and Head, Department of Management studies, Madurai Kamaraj University, one of the pioneers in the field of Management Education.

My sincere thanks to the Management of K.L.N.College of Engineering, **Shri.K.N.K.Ganesh**, President, **Shri S.V.S.Shivnath**, Secretary,

Shri.K.N.K. Karthik, Vice President, **Dr.S.Ganapathy**, Principal, **Prof.PL.Meiyappan,**

Director, **Prof L.V.Mohan**, Vice-principal and **Dr. T.K. Mahendra Babu** Dean (ARD) for their effective guidance.

My beloved husband **Mr. S. Raju**, Proprietor, Asir Consultants, Madurai, and my loving son **Master Dishan** deserve a special word of appreciation for their unstinted co-operation right from the beginning.

My special thanks to Dr.Ms.R.Vijailakshmi Stephen, Managing Director, Vijailakshmi Computers (P) Ltd., Madurai, who gave me useful suggestions throughout the preparation of this manuscript.

My sincere thanks to my **beloved parents, my sisters, and my family members** for having helped me in all possible ways and also for their deep concern and interest in my academic progress.

My joy knows no bounds to thank **Master Deva Prabhu** and **Baby Jerusha**, for having helped me with smiles and prayers.

CONTENTS

Chapter - 1

Historical Development

1.1 Introduction

Management is an exciting subject because it deals with setting, seeking and reaching objectives. We are all managers of our own lives, and the practice of management is found in every face of human activity like schools, business, churches, governments, unions and families. Peter F.Drucker has stated in his famous book **"THE PRACTICE OF MANAGEMENT"** that "The emergence of management as an essential, a distinct and leading social institution is a pivotal event in social history.

1.2 Definitions

Donald J.Clough

"Management is the art and science of decision making and leadership"

Joseph L. Massie

"Management is the process by which a co-operative group directs actions towards common goals"

Louis Allan

"Management is what a manager does"

F.W Taylor

"Management is the art of knowing what you want to do and then seeing that it is done in the end cheapest way"

The American Management Association

"The art of getting things done through other people"

Koontz and O'Donnel

"It is the art of getting the work done through and with people in formally organized groups"

Meaning of Management

Management is the art of getting things done by a group of people with the effective utilization of available resources. A minimum of two persons are essential to form a management

1.3 Is Management a Science or an Art

Management as a science

A science may be defined as "representing knowledge gathered by an observation and experiment, critically tested, systematized and brought under general principles."

It is true that management is not a science in the same way as biology; chemistry and astronomy as a science. It is also true that while it is easy to demonstrate the practical value of natural sciences, the same cannot be said of management, in the sense that it cannot cure a heart disease, or put people on the moon. But it would be wrong to say that management is beyond the reach of scientific study.

Management as a science refers to the application of scientific method in making decisions and evaluating different courses of action. It involves obtaining of complete, valid and reliable information in respect of the problem under consideration, before making a decision. The purpose of this exercise is to remove as far as possible the influence of personal preference or prejudice on the decision-making process.

The scientific decision-making process works as follows:

1. **Identification of the problem.** It involves correct recognition of a business problem before attempting a solution. The problem may relate to marketing of business, dealing with production delays, ensuring supplies of raw materials, excessive expenditure, or wastage etc., even a correct solution to a wrong problem may serve no purpose and if implemented, it may lead to undesirable consequences.

2. **Scientific inquiry.** It seeks to examine and evaluate alternative courses of action to resolve a given problem, taking into account the factors relevant to the problem and development of solutions.

3. **Choice of the best available alternative.** After analyzing the problem from all angles by using quantitative and non-quantitative techniques, duly taking into account the resource position of the business, the best available alternative is selected to resolve the problem.

4. **Rigorous control procedure:** By introduction of a strict control procedure to serve as a further check on the correctness of the original decision, it is ensured that the subsequent course of events is exactly as expected from the decision.

5. **Validity of principles.** Scientific methods and techniques are being increasingly applied to solve

business problems. Problems of a numeric nature (quantitative) are commonly solved through computers using problem-solving packages. It is equally common to develop mathematical and statistical models for the purpose.

Conclusion: Management is a field of knowledge that seeks to systematically understand **why and how men work together to accomplish the stated objectives and to make the co-operative efforts more useful to mankind.**

Management as an art

An art may be defined as "**a skill or knowledge in a particular field of activity, or a method of doing a thing**".

While it is true that in management these days, number of scientific techniques and method have been developed to facilitate decision making, but these techniques can be used only in respect of a problem of a numeric quantitative nature. But all the problems relating to management are not of a numeric nature, but relate to people. Problems of this type can only be resolved by applying **past experience, common sense, managerial skill and human understanding.** And it is this part of decision-making that raises management to the level of an art.

The art of management places particular emphasis on the following attributes:

1. **Past experience:** Experience is the sum total of knowledge, skill and practice derived from direct observation of, or participation in, events. Only theoretical knowledge about the principles of management may not equip the manager to tackle the problem relating to working with groups of people. The manager is basically concerned with performance

on the part of his subordinates in the pursuit of organizational goals. He should be able to guide his subordinates towards the goals, he should be able to understand, predict and control their behavior such that they identify their individual goals with the goals of the organization as a whole. But knowledge of individual and group behavior can only be gained in the school of life, by direct observation and participation.

2. The manager with a **common sense** can achieve his objectives of maximum productivity and profitability by proper arrangement, placement and timing of lifeless objects like money, materials, machines etc.,

3. **Managerial skills.** The functions of management include

   a. Establishment of the overall purpose or policy of the organization

   b. Planning and forecasting

   c. Organization of work, allocation of duties and responsibilities

   d. Giving instructions or orders

   e. Checking performance according to plan and

   f. Coordination of work of others.

4. **Human understanding:** The manager has an opportunity to control other human beings i.e., his subordinates. He take decisions on behalf of others who on their part have little or no influence on decision-making, and are therefore either forced to

comply with the decisions made by him or to leave the organization.

Therefore it requires a great deal of creativity and imagination on the part of the management to make the employees realize that achievement of organizational goals would ultimately result in the achievement of their personal goals and ensure for the increased pay packets, security of jobs, status and self-confidence. Only a manager with deep understanding of human behavior would be able to know the needs and motives which have brought his subordinates to work for the organization.

Conclusion: Any art has three essential components, namely the artist's vision, knowledge of craft and successful communication. An artistic skill can be developed through training. Management possesses all these components and can rightly be described as an art.

1.4 Management is Both—a Science and an Art

If science enables one to know, art enables one to do.

Management may be said to be a unique combination of science and art, it requires knowledge of the science of management i.e., the theory or principles of management which have been developed by thinkers and practitioners of management after years of experimentation. Knowledge of the science of management will enable the manager to correctly identify the issues and problems facing him, and to determine the course of action, which will best meet the situation. It is at this point that the art of management takes over. The manager can successfully perform a job only if he is able to identify and diagnose the problems correctly and apply his knowledge to solve them in a manner, which is the best under the given circumstances.

1.5 Differences between a Science and an Art

S.No	Science	Art
1.	It develops by knowledge	It develops practice acquired through observation and Experimentation.
2.	It explains the cause-effect Relationships between variables.	Cause-effect relationships cannot always be seen and the explanation is subjective based on the person's own under-standing and interpretation.
3.	It lays down universal laws and principles, which remain valid in all situations.	The laws and principles are not of universal nature and their validity will differ from situation to situation.
4.	It predicts on the basis of knowledge of relationships between variables.	It is merely a guess based on subjective understanding of realities.
5.	It is definitive.	It is descriptive.

The person should know where he wants to go and also know how to reach there, but if he does not take the first step, or falters on the way due to lack of will, he will never be able to accomplish his goals. The art of management consists in choosing one out of the many alternative courses of actions and to achieve the end-results through adaptations and adjustments that may be necessary on the way.

1.6 Management as a Profession

A profession is defined as a "calling or occupation that serves others, then management may be said to be a profession". But a profession is defined as a "vocation requiring specialized knowledge and long and intensive academic preparation". Such as the profession of a doctor or a lawyer or a chartered accountant, in these days it is common to find universities and professional bodies imparting knowledge and training in various branches of management and people with such knowledge and training are widely preferred for managerial jobs in organizations.

1. Body of knowledge

The study of management is multi-disciplinary because the subject draws heavily on **Sociology, Social Psychology, Economics, Commerce, Geography, Anthropology**, and so on. With the passage of time, certain concepts of management have been developed and there is a vast amount of technical information relating to specialized management areas such as production, marketing, finance and personnel. To be a successful manager, familiarity with these concepts is necessary.

2. Social obligation

Like a doctor or a lawyer, a manager is also engaged in serving the society, in the sense that he uses scarce resources for production of socially useful goods and services.

3. License of degree

Unlike a doctor or a lawyer, no license or degree as such is required to become a manager. But people with knowledge and training in the field of management are widely preferred for managerial jobs.

4. Code of conduct

Unlike members of other recognized professions, such as medicine or law, managers have no enforceable code of conduct, though the Indian Management Association has prescribed certain obligations, such as non-disclosure of employer's trade secrets, abstaining from making any personal gain at the expense of the employer Working for social good, and so on.

Conclusion

It is good that it is not formally recognized as a profession because in the case of management, the emphasis is rightly on performance rather than on academic training.

Fayol's Contribution

Fayol also proposed 14 principles of administration which he believed would be most often applied. These principles have been regarded as characteristics of a formal organization of bureaucracy as laid down by Max Weber. These 14 principles are not exhaustive by any means but are used most frequently. Based on the five functions of management, Fayol proposed fourteen universally accepted principles of management.

1. ***Division of work:*** This means that a worker is given only a small element of work to do, in which he becomes a specialist. Specialization leads to better efficiency and maximum output. This can be applied to all kinds of work, technical as well as managerial.

2. ***Authority and Responsibility:*** Authority is the right to command to get the work done. The responsibility is the accountability of authority so that the official authority is not misused.

3. ***Discipline:*** Fayol considered discipline as, outward marks of respect observed in accordance with the employment agreements and organizational rules. These rules and agreements should be clearly defined and understood. Also, these rules and regulations should be enforced fairly and judiciously.

4. ***Unity of command:*** Everyone should have only one superior, otherwise conflict and confusion in authority and instructions would result.

5. ***Unity of Direction:*** Activities having a common objective should be supervised by one supervisor with one plan of action. For instance, the book keeping department in an organization should not have two or more supervisors each with different policies and procedures.

6. ***Subordination of individual interest to the general interest:*** The interest of one employee or group of employee should not prevail over that of company or broader organization.

7. ***Remuneration of Personnel:*** Compensation for work done by organization members should be fair and satisfactory to both the employees and the organization.

8. ***Centralization:*** Centralization refers to the role of subordinates in decision making. The objective should be to make optimum utilization of the talents of personnel while retaining final responsibility for management.

9. ***The scalar chain:*** The communication should follow the formal channel in the hierarchy. The line of authority should run in order of rank from the top management to the lowest level in the enterprise. Fayol solved this problem by introducing the ***Gang Plank Policy,*** where such people could communicate with

each other directly, but with the permission of their superiors. For example, in the scalar chain, below, E would have to ascent the hierarchy to A and descend to K in order to pass a lateral message.

A
B H
C I
D J
E K
F L
G M

The Gang Plank principle avoids this problem so that E and K can get together to discuss the issues.

10. ***Order:*** **A place for everything and everything in its place.** This order required precise knowledge of the human requirements and the resources of the concern and a constant balance between their requirements and their resources. The workers and the material should be in the right place at the right time, for maximum efficiency.

11. ***Equity:*** Managers should be both fair and friendly to the subordinates. Equity results when friendliness is coupled with justice. The application of the principle of equity requires good sense, experience and good nature. This will help in soliciting loyalty and devotion from subordinates.

12. ***Stability of staff:*** Employee turnover should be minimized. Tenure and long term commitment should be encouraged. It results in a sense of belonging to the organization giving rise to dedication and better output.

13. ***Initiative:*** Subordinates should be encouraged to initiate new ideas and carry out their plans, even when some mistakes result.

14. ***Esprit de corps:*** The employees should work as a team because there is strength in unity and the management should promote this team spirit.

Review questions

Two mark questions

1. Define Management?
2. What do you mean by Management as a Science?
3. What do you mean by Management as an Art?
4. Highlight the differences between Science and an Art?
5. Define Profession? Give a few examples?
6. What is Code of Conduct?
7. Explain the following terms with an example?

   a)Division of work b)Authority and Responsibility

   c) Unity of command d) Unity of direction

   e) Centralization f) Scalar chain
8. What do you mean by Esprit de corps?

Part - B

1. Comment on the true nature of management. Is it a science or an art?

2. "Management is getting things done through others" Elaborate?

3. What are the attributes of a profession? Is management a profession? Is it necessary for every business to have a professional management?

Chapter - 2

Functions of Management

2.1 Functions of Management

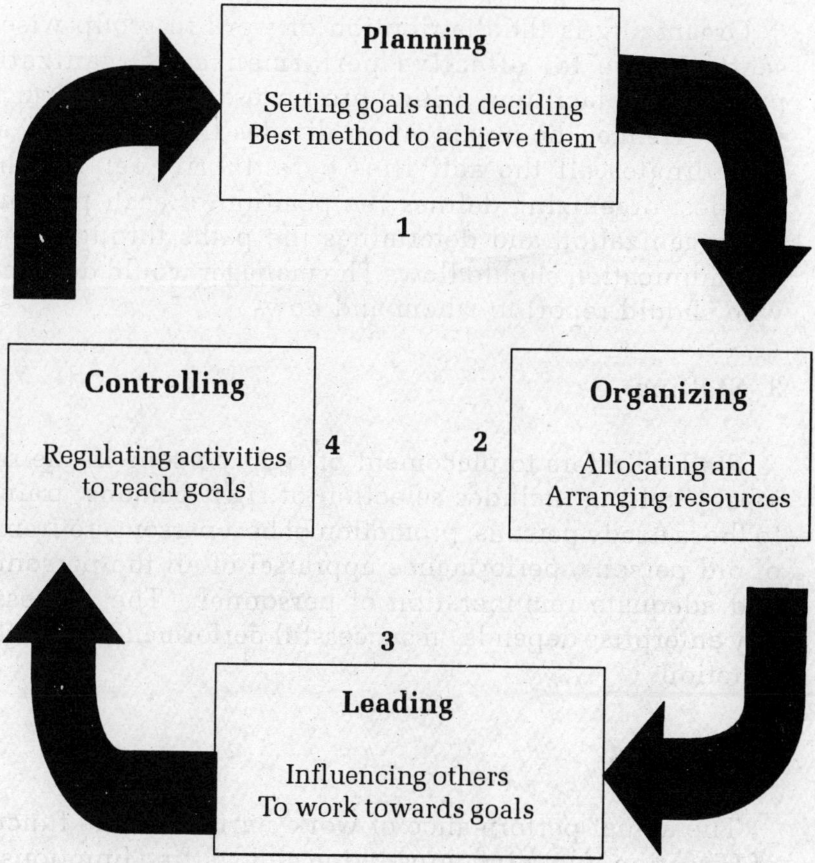

1. Planning

Planning is the primary function of management. Nothing can be performed without planning. In short, planning refers

to deciding in advance that which will be done in the near future. In order to achieve objectives, the organization plans what is to be done, when it is to be done, how it is to be done, and by whom it is to be done. Planning should take place before doing; most individual or group efforts are made by determining before any operative action takes place, what shall be done, where, how and who shall do it".

2. Organizing

Organizing is the distribution of work in group wise or section wise for effective performance. Organization provides all facilities, which are necessary to perform the work. Hence, the organization divides the total work and co-ordinates all the activities by authority relationship. Besides, organizing defines the position of each person in the organization and determines the paths through which communication should flow. The manager would determine who should report to whom and how.

3. Staffing

Staffing refers to placement of right persons in the right jobs. Staffing includes selection of right persons, training to those needy persons, promotion of best persons, retirement of old persons, performance appraisal of all the personnel, and adequate remuneration of personnel. The success of any enterprise depends on successful performance of staffing function.

4. Directing

The actual performance of work starts with the function of Direction. Planning, organizing and staffing functions are concerned with the preliminary work for the achievement of organizational objectives. Direction includes guidance, supervision and motivation of employees. It is the final action of a manager in getting others to act after all preparations have been completed.

5. Coordinating

All the activities are divided group wise or section wise under organizing function. Now, such grouped activities are coordinated toward the accomplishment of objectives of an organization. The difficulty of co-ordination depends upon the size of organization.

6. Motivation

The goals are achieved with the help of motivation. Motivation includes increasing the speed, performance of work and developing willingness on the part of workers. The workers expect favorable climatic conditions to work, fair treatment, monetary or non-monetary incentive and effective communication and gentleman approach.

7. Controlling

Controlling function ensures that the achieved objectives conform to pre-planned objectives. Necessary corrective action may be taken if there is any deviation. The control is very easy whenever the organization has a fixed standard. A good system of control has the characteristics of economy, flexibility, understanding and adequacy to organizational needs.

8. Decision-making

Every employee of an organization has to take a number of decisions every day. Decision-making helps in the smooth functioning of an organization.

9. Communication

Communication is the transmission of human thoughts, views or opinions from one person to another person. Workers are informed about what should be done, where it is to be done, how it is to be done and when it is to be done.

Communication helps the regulation of job and co-ordinate the activities.

Henry Fayol classifies the functions of management as forecasting, planning, organizing, commanding, coordinating and controlling. Luther Gullik classifies the functions of management as:

POSDCORB where

P	-	Stands for Planning,
O	-	for Organizing,
S	-	for Staffing,
D	-	for Directing,
C_o	-	for coordinating,
R	-	For Reporting and
B	-	for Budgeting.

2.2 Importance of Management

1. Management meet the challenge of change
2. Accomplishment of group goals
3. Effective utilization of business
4. Effective functioning of business
5. Resource development
6. Sound organization structure

7. Management directs the organization

8. Integrates various interests

2.3 Social Responsibility and Social Audit

Once the aim of all firms was to produce more and more and to make great profits at any cost and by any means. Maximization of profit was only a guiding factor. Now, business is not only a pursuit of profits out of the satisfaction of the needs of the consumer but also it is a social function involving certain obligations.

Needs for Social Responsibilities of Business:

- Corporations are culture of society and shou. d therefore respond to the demands of the society.

- The long-run self interests of business are best served. When business assumes social responsibilities.

- It is the normal and right thing to do.

Meaning of Social Responsibilities of Business

Business Units are the creatures of the society. The business operations are controlled and watched by the Government, share holders, consumers etc. So that, the firm should keep the interests of different people in the society, like consumers, Government, and employees in their minds. It is nothing but the total obligations of the business unit to the society.

Factors determining Social Responsibilities of Business

- Fear of Nationalization

- Intervention of Trade Union Movement

- Spread of business education
- Development of consumer councils
- Other moral, social, ethical and economic forces.

Kinds of Social Responsibilities

Social responsibilities of business may be grouped into two broad categories.

1. **Internal Social Responsibilities**
   a. Obligations to owners (shareholders)
   b. Obligations to employees
2. **External Social Responsibilities**
   a. Obligations to Consumers
   b. Obligations to Government
   c. Obligations to Community

H.S Singhania classifies the nature of social responsibility of business into two categories.

1. The manager in which a business carries out its own business activity and
2. The welfare activity that it takes upon itself as an additional function for E.g. a business should obey all the laws it should provide the maximum quality goods, pay tax, pay a fair wages to employees in addition to its commercial activities, business should also play a role in promoting social welfare activities. E.g. addressing the importance of family planning in the village areas.

Obligations to owners (shareholders)

The owners of business may be proprietors, shareholders and partners who invest their money in business for making profit or fair return on their investment. So, the business should be managed efficiently so as to provide a fair return on the investment and capital appreciation. The firm should send periodical reports about its working for its owners.

Obligations to employees

Responsibilities of business enterprise towards employees are as follows:

1. Wages to the workers should be need-based.

2. Salaries to the staffs should be linked with responsibility risk-taking, initiative and skill.

3. The Employees must be given security of service

4. Workers must be given equal chance for growth and development.

5. The employees ought to be provided healthy and satisfactory working conditions.

6. There must be good employee welfare and social security schemes.

Obligations to Consumers

The consumer is the king or deciding authority of any business. The obligations to them are given below:

1. Consumers of different classes, tastes and purchasing power should be satisfied through different goods by the firms.

2. The prices of the goods should be reasonable.

3. Goods to be of dependable quality and of sufficient variety.

4. After sales service

5. Wide spread distribution of goods and services among all sections of consumers.

6. Misleading Advertisements not to be given.

7. Prevention of Monopoly.

8. Consumers should be treated in a courteous manner.

Obligation to Government

Business firms have to extend their co-operation to implement the government policies and programmes. It should help the government regarding.

1. Equitable distribution of income and wealth

2. Fair price scheme

3. Anti-inflationary action

4. Tax policies etc.

5. To be a law-binding firm

6. To pay the dues fully and honestly

7. Not to corrupt public servants

8. To sell their product without adulteration

9. To maintain fair trade practices

Obligations to Community

Community means the society which includes consumers, government, investors, companies, employees etc. The business firm should not only focus their gains on any one of the groups in a society but also on all, in simple words, the fruits of the business firm should be equally distributed to the people in the society. It should provide amenities to the people and the locality where it is located. The firm should pay their taxes and fees regularly and honestly to the government. Because these funds have to be utilized for the welfare of the society by the government. So, the business community must try to provide the maximum possible services.to the population and remedy to national problems such as unemployment, over population, rural development, environmental protection, control of pollution etc.

These responsibilities includes

1. Taking appropriate steps to prevent environmental pollution and to preserve the ecological balance
2. Assisting in the over all development of the locality
3. Taking steps to conserve scare resources and developing alternatives, where possible
4. Improving the efficiency of the business operation
5. Development of backward areas
6. Promotion of small-scale industries
7. Contributing the national effort to build up a better society.

2.4 Social Audit

Every business unit has obligation to its employees, owners, buyers, government, environment, disadvantaged people and others. It goes to the credit of businessmen that they have understood their obligations and have been discharging them ably.

Nature of social Audit

A social Audit is a systematic study and evaluation of an organization's social performance. It is concerned with the possible influences on the social quality of life instead of the economic quality of life. Social audit leads to a report on the social performance of a business unit.

Features of Social Audit

(1) The areas for social audit include any activity which has a significant social impact, such as activities affecting environmental quality, consumerism, opportunities for women and other disadvantaged people in society and similar others.

(2) The second feature about social audit is that it can determine only what an organization is doing in social areas, not the amount of social good that results from these activities. It is a process audit rather than an audit for results.

(3) Thirdly, social performance is difficult to audit because most of the results of social activities occur beyond the company's gate and company has no means of securing data on the results.

(4) Finally social audits use both qualitative and quantitative data. The pressures to use quantitative approach are strong because of its repair ability

approvals respectability and apparent objectivity. Quantitative data are precise & convincing, but in the area of social philosophy and human values it is misleading to report only in quantitative terms. They can communicate only a part of the total situation, a part of the whole truth. Both quantitative & qualitative data are essential.

Activities Covered by Social Audit

A. Ecology and Environmental Quality

a) Clear up of existing pollution.

b) Design of processes to prevent pollution.

c) Aesthetic improvements.

d) Noise control

e) Dispersion of industry

f) Control of land use.

g) Required recycling.

B. Consumerism

a) Truth in labelling, in advertising, and in all business activities.

b) Product warranty and service.

c) Control of harmful products.

C. Community needs

a) Use of business expertise to solve community problems.

b) Reduction in role of business community and powei structure.

c) Aid with health care facilities.

d) Aid with urban renewal.

D. Governmental Relations

a) Restrictions on lobbying.

b) Control of business in political action.

c) Extensive new regulation of business.

d) Restrictions on international operations.

E. Business Giving

a) Financial support for artistic activities.

b) Donations to education.

c) Financial support for asserted charities.

F. Minorities and Disadvantaged Persons

a) Training of hard - core unemployment.

b) Operation of programmes for alcoholics and drug addicts.

c) Employment of persons with prison records.

G. Labor Relations

a) Improvement of occupational health and safety.

b) Expansion of employee rights.

c) Control of pensions, especially vesting of pension rights.

H. Shareholder Relations

a) Opening of boards of directors to members of public representing various interest groups.

b) Improvement of financial disclosure.

c) Disclosure of activities affecting the environment and social issues.

I. Economic Activities

a) Control of conglomerates.

b) Breakup of giant industry.

c) Restriction of patent use.

2.5 Evolution of social Audit

Social Audit is relatively a new development. Theodore Kreps who was the founding father of the idea, has summarized his findings in 72 industries spanning over 2 decades. He included among these measurements:

1. Employment.

2. Production.

3. Consumer effort commanded.

4. Consumer funds absorbed.

5. Pay rolls.

6. Dividends and interest.

Howard Bowen conducted an independent appraisal every 5 years by a group of auditors; he suggested 8 areas for appraisal:

(1) Price.

(2) Wages.

(3) Research and Development.

(4) Advertising.

(5) Public relations.

(6) Human relations.

(7) Community relations

(8) Employment stabilization.

Organization for social Audit

Social audit can be made by internal auditors, outside consultants, or a combination of the two. The internal auditor has the advantage of familiarity with the business, but his assessment might be influenced by his loyalty to the company. A consultant has the advantage of an outsides view but lacks familiarity with the company and he is likely to ignore significant data. A combination of the two is ideal for carrying on the audit of social performance.

Bowen's original proposal was that a social audit should be made by outside consultants for inside use only, and that is should be made only every five years.

Audit Programme

The social audit is a new concept. As a result there are very few guidelines for making it, and there is no standard procedure to follow. Most companies are at the beginning of the learning curve with social audits. They are starting to experiment with them, but they have only limited results. When companies do begin audit procedures, they tend to find that the process is more complex than originally contemplated. Everything is related to every thing else. In all this confusion Tata Iron and Steel Company (TISCO) did succeed in having a social audit.

2.6 Benefits of social audit

1. Social audit enables the company to take close look at itself and understand how far the company has lived up to its social objectives.

2. Related to the first benefit is the fact that social audit encourages greater concern for social performance through-out the organization.

3. Social audit provides data for comparing effectiveness of the different types of programmes.

4. Social Audit provides cost data on social programmes so that management can relate the data to budgets, available resources, company objectives, and projected benefits of programmes.

5. Social Audit provides information for effective response to external claimants that make demands on the organization. News reporters, welfare organization, and variety of others want to know what a business is doing in areas of their special interest, and a business needs to respond as effectively as possible. The social audit shows a business where it is vulnerable to public pressure and where its strengths lie.

Review questions

Two mark questions

1. What is POSDCORB stand for?

2. Highlight the importance of Management?

3. Define Social responsibility?

4. What is the need for Social responsibility?

5. Define Social audit?

6. Mention any three benefits of Social audit?

Part B

1. What do you mean by Social responsibility oı business? Can the social problems of our country be converted into business opportunities?

2. "In Indian conditions the Social responsibilities of business are more in theory than in practice". Do you agree with this statement or not? Explain

3. What is social audit? What are the needs and Features of Social audit?

4. Briefly explain the Functions of Management?

Chapter - 3

Business Ethics

3.1 Business Ethics

Definitions

Wright defines "Ethics is that branch of philosophy which is the systematic study of reflective choice of the standards of right or wrong by which it is to be guided and of the goods towards which it may ultimately be directed".

Webster defines ethics as "the discipline dealing with that which is good and bad and with moral duty and obligation.

Hurley defines "Ethics as a system of moral principles". Business ethics may be defined as a set of moral rules and principles to protect the interest of customers, employees, society, business unit and the industry as a whole.

Meaning

Business ethics means the behaviors of a business man while conducting a business, by observing morality in his business activities.

The business should pursue the following:

1. It should avoid discrimination on the basis of religion, caste, social status etc., in matters of providing employment to members of the community.
2. It should seek to develop healthy relations with the trade unions formed by its workers.

3. It should discharge its duties to the state by paying taxes in time and assisting it in ensuring balanced development of the country.

4. It should extend all help and support to social, religious, educational and charitable institutions.

5. It should avoid production of goods like tobacco, liquor, prohibited drugs which may create harm to the people.

6. It should take care that its production processes do not result in air or water pollution.

7. It should involve itself in the affairs of the community to enrich individual and social life.

A business, for example, can adopt one or more villages and by financial and technical help, assist in progress and prosperity of the poor and the needy.

3.2 Need for Business Ethics

1. Survival of the business unit

Businessmen should consider the interest of the business unit. Unethical practices of a businessman will lead to the closure of business unit. The closure of a business unit does not only create problems to business but also to employees and the society in general.

2. Growth of business unit

Whenever a businessman observes ethics strictly, definitely the particulars business unit will get developed. A business could not be run in such a manner as is detrimental to the interest of society or business itself. So, it is argued that there should be some business ethics for the growth of a business.

3. Earning goodwill

The prime objective of any business is to earn profit. At the same time, no business is allowed to earn profit without following business ethics. If business ethics are properly followed by a business, automatically that particular business unit earns a good name among the public.

4. Improving the confidence

Business ethics are necessary to improve the confidence of the customers, employees and the like. If confidence is infused, they (customers and employees) will popularize the name or excellent consumer services of the particular business unit.

5. Maintaining Inter-relationship

No business functions separately or independently. Each business has close relationship with another business even though the nature and size of the other business differs. It is expected that each business unit should have a smooth relationship with others. The inter-relationship of business is maintained by adopting business ethics.

6. Solving social problems

If a businessman observes ethics in his business, the public have no difficulty in having their wants fulfilled. There is no bargaining between the businessman and public. There is a fair treatment of an employee by him. This will avoid social problems like strike, lockout, etc.

3.3 Principles of Business Ethics

Following are some of the basic principles of business ethics. They are briefly explained:

1. Service motive should be in the first place rather than profit motive, even though the very purpose of any business is to earn profits.
2. There is no discrimination against any particular group of people, say the rich, the poor, the high, the low, the caste, the religion, etc.,
3. Fullest satisfaction should be available to consumers.
4. There is no lack of consideration for clean environment.
5. Human feelings are properly considered while rendering service.
6. There is no wastage or misuse of available scarce resources.
7. Business must be dynamic and efficient.
8. Business should provide quality products at reasonable price.
9. Business must maintain or improve standard of living.
10. There must be healthy competition.
11. There should be job security to employees.
12. Businessman must be sincere in payment of fair wages.
13. Better working conditions or environment should be provided.

14. Efficient employees are properly motivated and recognized.
15. Employees are requested to participate in management.
16. Monetary and non-monetary incentives must be available to employees.
17. Businessman must pay taxes promptly and obey other obligations promptly.
18. Business unit must avoid unfair trade practices like hoarding, black-marketing etc.
19. There should be no formation of cartel agreements to control production, price, etc.
20. Businessman must disclose all relevant information to needy persons.
21. Businessman must prepare genuine books of accounts and presents before all authorized persons as and when required by them.
22. He should protect the interests of its members at the time of amalgamations, absorption and the like.
23. He should be ready to extend mutual co-operation and mutual help.
24. Business should act as a partner in the development of nation.
25. He should follow proper communication system at the levels.
26. He should not make promises that could not be fulfilled.

27. Business assets should not be utilized by it owner or employees for personal use.

28. Employees are allowed free speech in the work place.

29. Business unit should follow proper personnel policy with regard to promotion, transfer and the like.

30. Businessman should not indulge in politics.

3.4 Benefits of Business Ethics

A business may be conducted according to certain self-recognized business ethics. If so, certainly, the following benefits are available to the concerned groups. The benefits of business ethics are listed group wise:-

1. Customer

1. Receive quality goods.

2. Pay reasonable price.

3. No difficulty in obtaining goods.

4. No price discrimination.

5. No price fluctuation.

2. Employees

1. Fair wages.

2. Better working conditions and working environment.

3. Recognizing human feelings.

4. Reward for efficiency.

5. Job security.
6. Participation in management.
7. Proper personnel policy.

3. Industry

1. Healthy competition.
2. Better co-operation and co-ordination.
3. Steady growth.

4. Business

1. Adequate Profit.
2. Fast growth
3. Fast diversification of business.
4. Less labour turnover.

5. Society

1. Better utilization of resources.
2. Improving standard of living.
3. No pollution problem.

6. Government

1. Prompt collection of taxes.
2. Development of nation.
3. Easy implementation of legislation.

Review Questions

Two Mark Questions

1. Define Business ethics?
2. Give a few examples of ethics?
3. Why should the Business pursue ethics?
4. Highlight any three benefits of ethics for

   a)Customer b)Employees c)Business

   d)Industry e)Government f)Society

PART – B

1. Briefly explain the Principle of business ethics?
2. Explain the need for business ethics?

Chapter - 4

Planning

4.1 Introduction

Planning is essential in every walk of life. Each and every person has to frame a plan to proceed in his scheme. Planning is the primary function of management. As a process it involves the conscious determination of future course of action in order to achieve the desired results. Planning determines the time of action to achieve the predetermined organizational goals. It answers six pertinent questions i.e. **what, why, where, How, Who and when?** It seeks the answer in advance. What should be done? Why is action necessary? Where, When and how should it be done? And who shall do it? It is a process of thinking before doing.

4.2 Definitions and Meaning

Koontz and O'Donnel

"Planning is deciding in advance what to do, how to do it, when to do it and who is to do it. It bridges to gap from where we are to where we want to go"

Terry

Planning is the selecting and relating of facts and the making and using of assumptions regarding the future in the visualization and formulation of proposed activities believed, necessary to achieve desired results.

W.H.Newman

"Planning is deciding in advance what is to be done, that is a plan is a projected course of action"

Allen

"A plan is trap laid to capture the future".

J.P.Barger

"Planning is an ability to visualize a future process and its results"

M.S.Aurley

"Planning is deciding in advance what is to be done. It involves the selection of objectives, policies, procedures and programmes from among alternatives".

Kast & Rosenzweig

" A plan is a determined course of action

H. Fayol

"Planning is deciding the best alternatives among others to perform different managerial operations in order to achieve the pre-determined goals.

Hamilton Church

"Planning is in essence, that exercise of foresight".

Hodge and Johnson

" Planning is an attempt to anticipate the future in order to achieve better performance"

Meaning :

It is an intellectual process of thinking resorted to decide a course of action, which helps to achieve the pre-determined objectives of the organization in future.

Plans

A Plan is the means devised for attempting to reach a goal. A manager should plan all his managerial functions effectively. Plan provides the standard and degree of control. Goals and plans are closely related. Goals are the desired results whereas the plans are the means to bring about these results. The plan period may be short or long. Depending on the duration or period, the plan can be categorized into three different types.

1. Short Range Plans - Up to 1 year
2. Intermediate Range Plans - 1 to 5 years and
3. Long Range plans - Above 5 years

4.3 Characteristics of Planning

The following are the main characteristics of planning

1. Planning is looking into the future.
2. Planning involves Pre-determined line of action
3. Planning discovers the best alternative out of available many alternatives.
4. Planning requires considerable time for implementation.
5. Planning is a continuous process.
6. Planning object is to achieve pre-determined objectives in a better way.
7. Planning integrates various activities of organization.

8. Planning is done for a specific period.

9. Planning not only selects the objectives but also develops policies, programmes, and procedures to achieve the objectives.

10. Planning is required at all levels of management.

11. Planning is an inter-dependent process which co-ordinates the various business activities.

12. Planning directs the members of the organization.

13. Growth and prosperity of any organization depends upon planning

4.4 Nature and Purpose of Planning

1. Planning is Primary

The functions of management include planning, organizing, staffing, directing and controlling. Writers of the management unanimously accept that planning is the primary function of all the other functions. The reason is that the manager wants to achieve the pre-determined objectives in a better way.

2. A thinking Process

It is an intellectual exercise. It is concerned with thinking in a creative way as to how the existing combination of resources may be adjusted and adopted to match the emerging opportunities.

3. Planning is flexible

While planning any activity, any one of the available

alternatives is selected. Planning selects the best alternative based on certain assumptions. If the assumptions are proved wrong, the selected alternative tends to be an incorrect one and vice-versa.

4. Planning is a continuous Process

Planning does not come to an end with the establishment of a business concern. A number of decisions are taken during the lifetime of the business concern. So, planning is necessary throughout the running of business concern as a continuous process.

5. Unity and Consistency

Every department manager resorts to planning at different times. Managerial actions of different managers are unified in order to achieve the objectives. Policies and procedures of the organization provide a basis for the consistency of executive behavior and action in matters of planning.

6. Planning is common to all

Planning work is done by every person who is working in a business unit. He may be a managing director or a foreman.

7. Basis for all managerial functions

Planning is found at all levels of management. Top management looks after strategic planning, middle management looks after administrative planning and the lower level management looks after operational planning.

8. Getting Co-ordination

Planning co-ordinates various business activities. Without planning, nothing can be coordinated.

9. Considering limiting factors

Every plan is formulated after considering the limiting factors. It may be money, skilled labor, quality materials, plant and machinery.

4.5 Purpose of Planning

1. Primacy of Planning

Planning logically precedes all other managerial functions i.e. organizing, staffing directing and controlling.

2. Focusing attention on objectives

Organizations exist to pursue and achieve certain objectives. Planning focuses on these objectives. It directs action for achieving these objectives. Planning defines these objectives more clearly and determines the course of action to achieve them.

3. Eliminating Uncertainty and change.

Planning helps in reducing uncertainties of future. A significant aspect of it is to obtain information to forecast conditions in future. In order to cope with the business changes, the organization must look ahead for its future course of action, which is basically provided by planning process. Planning does not stop changes in the environment. It gears the organization to cope with the changed situation in order to achieve the objectives.

4. Providing the Basis for control

There can be no real control without planning. Some control is necessary to see that events conform to plans. It is exercised in the context of planning. Without planning it is not possible.

5. Helping co-ordination

Managerial functions in an organization require co-ordination for which beginning is made at planning stage. Various departments work in accordance with the overall plans to achieve harmony. Co-ordination is the essence of management. Planning is its basic condition.

6. Minimizing cost of performance

Planning gives an even flow of work without any fiction of energy for consistency and balance of efforts. It removes hesitancy, avoids crisis, eliminates false steps and protects against improper deviations. Planning involves a lot of time, money and energy in the formulation. If it is formulated and implemented in right earnest, it yields impressive results.

7. Basis for Decentralization

To delegate authority the superiors should know well in advance how to delegate and make decisions. It becomes possible through planning to delegate the authority because one feels confident about how a subordinate will use his authority.

4.6 Steps in Planning

1. Opportunity analysis

An awareness of the factors in the external environment, the strength and the weaknesses is the first step in planning. What is our market, what is our competition, what are our customers' preferences, taste, what are our strengths and weaknesses.

2. Establishing objectives

"Where we want to be, and what we want to accomplish

and when" are answered in this step. Objectives are set for the organization and each subordinate is also entrusted with it. Objectives give us the expected results and where the primary emphasis is to be placed. For example if an enterprise wants to have its objective as Rs.200 crores the next year from now, then the departmental objectives are fixed and they are further divided into subordinate manager's goals etc. The goal setting normally emanates from the top. But it may also originate from the bottom.

Steps in Planning :

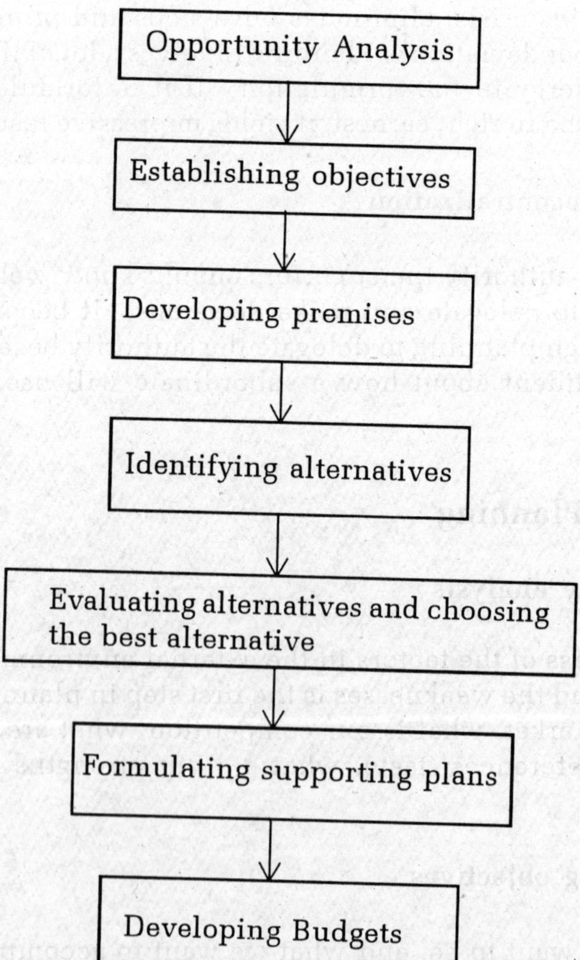

3. Developing premises

Premises are 'Assumptions' about the 'environment' It involves identification of critical factors of the environment that affect the planning

Examples of critical factors are government policies, tax rates, business cycle developments, economic indicators, economic forecasts etc. No body can precisely predict the environmental factors accurately and make an accurate forecast of future. However one can fairly predict the critical factors required for the plan.

4. Identifying alternatives

Every plan has got a set of alternative course of action. A reasonable number of alternatives can be developed for a plan.

5. Evaluating alternatives and selecting the best

A reasonable number of alternatives can be evaluated on the basis of the principle of limiting factor. The limiting factors may be costs, time, manpower, and other resources. By applying techniques of operations research, every alternative can be evaluated. For e.g. Alternative 'A; may benefit the organization in the short term but may be more expensive and alternative 'B' may benefit in the long run but may be less expensive. If one wants to earn immediate profits by spending more money he can choose alternative 'A';. If the limiting factor is cost, he is forced to choose alternative 'B'.

6. Formulating supportive plans

Planning is not complete with selecting the best alternative, a set of derivative plans are developed to support the basic plan. For e.g. An educational institution might like to own a fleet of buses, for which derivative plans for selection, training of drivers and maintenance. Staff are supportive plans for the main plan - procurement of buses.

7. Developing budgets

A numerated plan is a budget. Budget is referred in financial terms and they are required to control the plans.

4.7 Merits of Planning

1. Planning enables the enterprise to make adequate adjustment to adopt the future changes.
2. Because of pre-selected objectives and the direction of coordinated efforts achievement of goals becomes easier.
3. Since all the activities are in coordinated and in systematic way, the efficiency of the enterprise increases.
4. Planning helps management to adopt modern methods and technology to improve quality and to attract customer.
5. Planning enables an enterprise to be competent.
6. Planning provides adequate vision to the management. This eliminates any possibility of mistakes.
7. Planning increases the morale and confidence of managers so as to load effectively.
8. Planning involves considering other alternatives examining them.
9. Planning eliminates wastages and other time consuming process.
10. Planning is a process by which a manager can anticipate the future threats and discover alternative course of action open to him.

4.8 Demerits of Planning

1. Planning is based on assumptions; it cannot predict the future accurately.
2. Planning is a costly function; small organizations cannot afford it as it puts financial burden on them.
3. It is difficult to accommodate any change once the planning is complete.
4. Planning does not provide any immediate solutions if any unavoidable circumstances arises.
5. Delay in action caused by planning may create misunderstanding.

4.9 Barriers in Planning

1. Changing environment is one of the important barriers, which makes planning more difficult since long term planning in such condition is not possible.
2. According to the changing environment the plans must be altered frequently.
3. Few managers' approach towards planning is negative. They think that planning is an unnecessary and time-consuming phenomenon.
4. The pressure in increasing the works is another potential barrier in planning. Daily burdens may deviate their attention from planning.
5. Poor preparation of line managers in terms of their planning knowledge and skills.
6. Effective planning sometimes fails if any staff dominates the planning process.

5

Review questions

Two mark questions

1. Give the meaning and any two definition of Planning?
2. What are the advantages of Planning?
3. What are the demerits of Planning?
4. What are the types of Planning?
5. What do you mean by Premises?

Part –B

1. Explain the characteristics of Planning?
2. Briefly explain the Nature and Purpose of Planning?
3. “Planning is essence of Management. It is a management function” Elucidate.
4. Planning is essentially forward looking? Explain in detail the business of Planning?
5. Explain the Steps in Planning?

Chapter - 5

Objectives

5.1 Definitions

MC Farland has defined "Objectives are the goals, aims or purposes that organizations wish to achieve over varying periods of time".

Terry has defined that "A managerial objective is the intended goal which prescribes definite scope and suggests direction to the efforts of a manager"

Koontz and O'Donnel "Objective is a term commonly used to indicate the endpoint of a management programme".

Meaning

It is the expectation of end results for which an organization is established and which it tries to achieve. The objective may differ from one organization to another organization.

5.2 Categories of Objectives

1. **Societal objectives:** which are concerned with creation and maintenance of cultural values through the production of goods and services.

2. **Output objectives:** concerned with the kind of output.

3. **System objectives:** Concerned with growth, stability, profitability and efficiency.

4. **Product objectives:** Concerned with quality, quantity innovativeness of the goods and services.

5. **Derived objectives:** Concerned with secondary areas. Example: Community development.

Features of Objectives

1. Each individual has objectives of his own. If the individuals collectively form into a group, the group has more than one objective. The created group tries to achieve these objectives.

2. The objectives of any organization are to be specifically mentioned. The objectives may be short or long term and broad or specific objective.

3. The objectives of an organization should be clearly defined. The clearly defined objectives are very much useful to the top executives for the sight direction of personnel.

4. At top level, the organization has broad objectives. The whole organization is divided into several sections. Each section has specific objectives. The marketing section has the objectives regarding achieving certain level of sales. All the sections try to achieve the broad objectives of the organization.

5. The objectives of the organization must conform to the general needs of the public.

6. All the organizations have several objectives at a time. The reason is that the objectives are necessary in the various areas of business. The objectives of business may be relation to marketing, profitability, productivity and the development of social responsibility.

7. The objectives of the organization may be changed in due course. The old objectives are replaced by the new ones. The policy of the government and the social changes are the main factors responsible for the changes in objectives.

8. The objectives are expressed in numerical terms. Say Rs. 2,500 to 10,000 units. The profit or sales may be expressed in rupees. This helps in measuring the actual performance done to realize the objectives.

9. The framed objectives should be achievable. They should be achievable and reasonable ones.

5.3 Management by Objectives (MBO)

MBO is a management system in which each member of the organization effectively participates and involves himself. This system gives full scope to the individual strength and responsibility. MBO harmonizes the goal of an individual with the organization's goal. It creates self-control and motivates the manager into action before somebody tells him to do something.

Prof. Reddin defines MBO as "The establishment of effective standards for managerial positions and the periodic conversion of those into measurable time bound objectives linked vertically and horizontally and with future planning".

5.4 Features of MBO

1. An attempt is made by the management to integrate the goals of an organization and individuals. This will lead to effective management

2. MBO tries to combine the long-range goals of an organization with short-range goals.

3. Management tries to relate the organization goals with society goals.

4. MBO emphasis is not only on goals but also on effective performance.

5. It pays constant attention to refining, modifying and improving the goals and changing the approaches to achieve the goals on the basis of experience.

6. It increases the organizational capability of achieving goals at all levels.

7. A high degree of motivation and satisfaction is available to employees through MBO.

8. Recognizes the participation of employees in goal setting process.

9. Aims at replacing the exercise of authority with consultations.

10. Encourages a climate of trust, goodwill and a will to perform.

Process of MBO

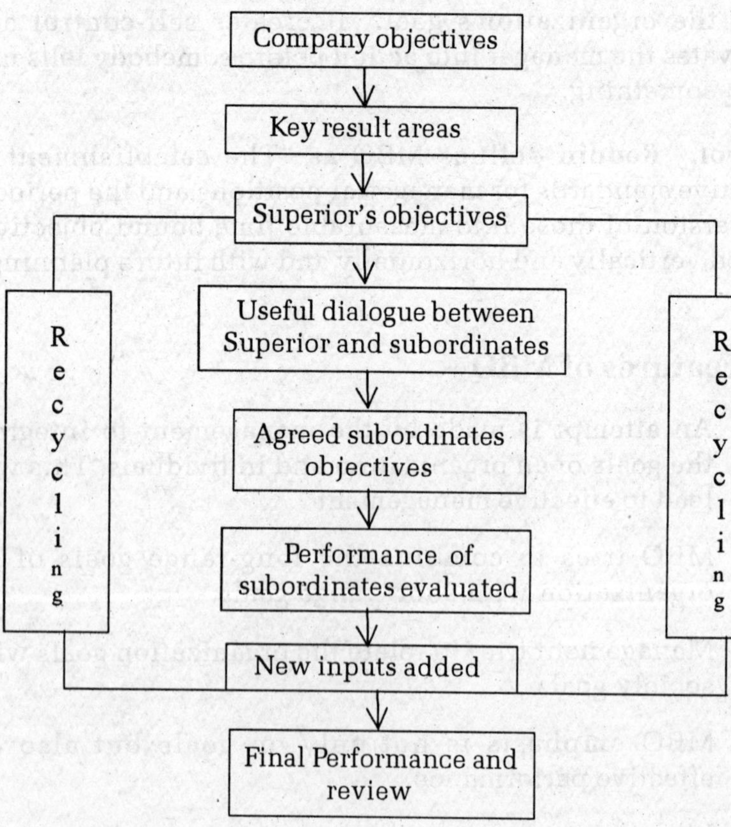

The balance of objectives of the organization and individual characterizes the MBO process. The process of MBO is explained below

1. Defining organizational objectives

Initially, organizational objectives are framed by the top-level employees of an organization. Then, it moves downwards. The definition organizational objectives state why the business is started and exists. First, long-term objectives are framed. Short-term objectives are framed taking into account the feasibility of achieving the long-term objectives.

2. Goals of each section

Objectives for each section, department or division are framed on the basis of overall objectives of an organization. Period within which these objectives should be achieved is also fixed. Goals or objectives are expressed in a meaningful manner.

3. Fixing key result areas

Key result areas are fixed on the basis of organizational objectives premises. Key Results Areas (KRA) are arranged on a priority basis. KRA indicates the strength of an organization. The examples of KRA are profitability, market standing, innovation etc.

4. Setting subordinate objectives or targets

The objectives of each subordinate or individual are fixed. It is preferable to fix the objectives at lower level in quantitative units. There should be a free and frank discussion between the superior and his subordinates. Subordinates are induced to set standards themselves by giving an opportunity. If subordinates are allowed to do so, they may set high standards and the chances of their accomplishment are higher. In this way, the objectives or targets of the subordinates are fixed.

5. Matching resources with objective

The objectives are framed on the basis of availability of resources. If certain resources (technical personnel or scarce raw material) are not adequately available, the objectives of an organization are changed accordingly. So, there is a need for matching resources' with objectives. Next, the available resources should be properly allocated and utilized.

6. Periodical review meetings

The superior and subordinates should hold meetings periodically in which they discuss the progress in the accomplishment of objectives. The fixed standards may be changed in the light of progress. But the basic conditions do not change. The periodical review meeting is held during the period set for achieving the objectives.

7. Appraisal of activities

At the end of the fixed period for achieving the objectives, there should be a discussion between the superior and subordinates. The discussion is related with subordinates' performance against the specified standards. The superior should take corrective action. According to Earl P. Strong, "Only by bringing company' objectives down from long range to short range, from company level to individual position level, from pre-performance to post-performance and by penalizing for failure and rewarding for success can be the effective programme of managing by objectives be accomplished."

The superior should identify the reasons for failure of achieving objectives. The problems faced by the subordinates should be identified-and steps should be taken to tackle such problems.

8. Reappraisal of objectives

An organization is living in a dynamic world. There are a lot of changes within short period. The survival and growth of a modern business organization largely depends upon putting up with the changing conditions. So, the top management executive should review the organization's objectives to frame the objectives according to the changing situation. According to Newman, summer and Wanen, "Every manager must frequently reappraise the emphasis he gives to his various objectives. The job is like that of a captain of a large ship who is continually changing his speed and direction in relation, to his present position, tides, winds and other conditions."

Benefits of MBO

The benefits of MBO are explained below:

1. Managers are involved in objectives setting at various levels of management under MBO and this commitment ensures hard work to achieve them.

2. MBO process helps the manager to understand their role in the total organization.

3. Manager recognizes the need for planning and appreciates the planning.

4. MBO provides a foundation for participative management. Sub-ordinates are also involved in goal setting

5. A department does not work at cross-purpose with another department. In other words, each department's objectives are consistent with the objectives of the whole organization.

6. Systematic evaluation of performance is made with the help of MBO.

7. MBO gives the criteria of performance. It helps to take corrective action

8. Delegation of authority is easily done with the help of MBO.

9. The practice of MBO helps the manager attend to job enrichment.

10. MBO motivates the workers by job enrichment and makes the jobs meaningful.

11. The responsibility of a worker is fixed through MBO.

12. Decision is taken by the management very quickly. The reason is that each worker knows the purpose of taking a decision and does not oppose the decision.

LIMITATIONS OF MBO

The limitations of MBO arise due to the application of the MBO.

1. MBO fails to explain the philosophy; most of the executives do not know how MBO works, what MBO is and why MBO is necessary and how participants can benefit by MBO.

2. MBO is a time consuming process. Much time is needed by senior people for framing the MBO. Next, it leads to heavy expenditure. Sometimes, managers are frustrated over MBO. MBO requires heavy paper work.

3. MBO emphasizes only on short-term objectives and does not consider the long-term objectives.

4. The status of subordinates is necessary for proper objectives setting. But, this is not possible in the process of MBO.

5. MBO is a rigid one. Objectives should be changed according to the changed circumstances, external or internal. If it is not done, the planned results cannot be obtained.

6. The objectives are set without considering the available resources.

Review questions

Two mark questions

1. Define objectives?

2. What do you mean by MBO?

3. What are the advantages of MBO?

4. What are the limitations of MBO?

Part –B

1. What do you mean by MBO? What are the different steps involved in it?

2. What are the Features of Objectives?

Chapter - 6

Strategies

6.1 Strategies

The word "strategy" is derived from the Greek word "strategy" meaning the office of the general. It is often used to mean the art of military leadership in the planning and execution of large-scale combat operations.

In managerial terminology, a strategy may be defined as "an overall plan for the organization, to accomplish its objectives in the context of environmental forces beyond the control of the organization," In other words, "strategy is concerned with an organization's relationship to the external environment and the competitive situation inherent therein. It seeks to lay down as to how the organization plans to meet the uncertain and competitive world outside, and makes different assumption as regards the tactics and strength of the competitors."

How strategy formulation is influenced by the environment

The external and internal environments of the organization influence formulation of a strategy. The external environment consists of opportunities, threats and constraints, and the internal environment reflects the strengths and weakness of the organization.

If the external environment is favorable, in the sense that it has a potential for expansion of goods and services, and if the organization has enough internal strengths in the form of physical, human and financial resources, its can go in for increasing the profitability by increased production of existing goods and services, diversification of activities either backwards towards the supply of necessary materials, or forwards towards sales markets, product development, and so on.

On the other hand, if the external environment indicates low opportunities for growth, then even with significant internal strengths, the organization will have to adopt a "hold tight" strategy awaiting a favorable external situation. And if neither external nor internal environment is favorable; the only advisable course of action would be to adopt the strategy of survival.

6.2 Types of Strategies

The following strategies may be adopted by an organization to accomplish its objectives:

1. Stability

In case the organization is satisfied with the present level of activities and profits, it may follow the 'stability strategy'. The factors which contribute to this line of approach may be: (a) stable environment; (b) limited number of the products and services; (c) limited number of customers, suppliers, and competitors; (d) minimum need for specialized knowledge and skills about products, customers, etc.; (e) values, attitudes, background, etc., of the top management which may disfavor growth for its own sake.

An important drawback of 'stability strategy' is that it may make the management complacent, find indifferent to the need for any change, such that when the external environment undergoes a swift change, the organization may not be fully prepared to bear its effects.

2. Product development

The main thrust of product development strategies is development of products for the existing markets and development of new products for new markets.

Product development strategy will be followed in case the

organization in response to dynamic environment decides to enter new products of services in the market in order to meet and beat the competitors more effectively.

Generally, product development strategies will be followed in the environment which is dynamic even to an extent unpredictable, with a large number of products, services, customers, suppliers and competitors.

3. Market development

Market development strategies are concerned with either selling the existing range of products in new markets, or selling new products in new market the underlying object in each case being to expand the customers being served by the existing products and services.

4. Vertical integration

Vertical integration is the process of consolidation, whereby an organization diversifies its activities either backward towards the supply of essential materials, or forwards towards sales outlets. Accordingly, It may decide to produce the necessary raw materials for its production activity so as to assure continuous supply. It may also decide to develop its own sales outlets in order to better serve the consumers.

Obviously, vertical integration strategies will be followed in response to a dynamic unpredictable environment-comprising a plenty of products and services, and a number of customers, suppliers and competitors.

5. Merger

Merger denotes the combining of several similar business units, so as to rationalize manufacturing and selling activities and to attain the economics of large-scale production and to weed out competition.

Merger as a strategy aims at acquiring other similar organization to expand products range and markets. Such a strategy will be followed in a dynamic unpredictable environment by an organization, which desires growth and expansion, without waiting for its own project to achieve the same results.

6. Divestment or retreat

To divest means to get rid of. In managerial terminology divestment as a strategy means to give up production of unprofitable products to achieve rationalization of the product range, and to avail the benefits of standardization. The products chosen for elimination are those, which contribute little or no profits. But the exercise should be undertaken with care, mind caution, because elimination of products with low profits may also adversely affect the overall profit position.

7. Other strategies

An organization may also adopt various other strategies. Such as distribution strategy, technological strategy, financial strategy, Managerial strategy, product design strategy, cost reduction strategy, etc., in order to accomplish its specific objectives.

Review questions

Two mark questions

1. Define strategies?
2. Explain the following term

   a)Stability — b)Merger

   c)Vertical integration — d) Divestment

Part – B

1. Briefly explain how Strategy Formulation is influenced by the Environment?

2. Briefly explain the Types of Strategies?

Chapter - 7

Policies

7.1 Definitions

Koontz and O'Donnell

"Policies were identified as guides to thinking in decision making. They assume when decisions are made and these will fall within certain boundaries."

George Terry

"Policy is a verbal, written or implied overall guide setting up boundaries that supply the general limits and direction in which managerial action will take place".

Characteristics of Policy

1. A guide to thinking in decision-making

Policy lays down the course of action selected to guide and determine present or future decisions. It should prove an effective instrument for the execution of plans to the organization.

2. Lays down the limits

Policy lays down limits within which decisions are to be made by the managers. Laying down limits assures consistent and unified actors and exercise of discretion on the part of those who have to implement it. The policy must be broad, general and flexible.

3. Framed by top level management

Policy may originate at any level such as division level, department, and section level, etc. A manager may formulate policies within the limits of his authority and also with in the limits of the policy lay down by his superiors.

4. Preceded by a brief description of subject matter

Policy starts with description of subject matter. It covers so that there may be common understanding of the policy among those who are to implement it.

5. May not be valid for all the time to come

A policy may be good in one set of circumstance. As the circumstances change, it is necessary that policy be reviewed periodically and modified according to the changed circumstances. It may be replaced by a new policy.

Essentials of Policy Formulation

1. It should be simple and easy to understand
2. It should be clearly defined and stated in understandable words.
3. It should help in achieving business objectives
4. It should be based on facts and not on guesswork.
5. It should be communicated to all those who are affected by it.
6. At the time of formulation of policy, people who are likely to be affected and who are responsible to implement it, should be consulted.

7. It should be flexible.
8. It should be realistic and attainable.
9. It should not be in conflict with other policies of the organization.
10. It should conform to economic principles.
11. It should take into consideration laws and regulations imposed by the government.
12. It should be compatible with public interest and social good.
13. It should cove all possible eventualities with which an organization is expected to be confronted in future.

7.2 Classification of Policies

1. Classification on the Basis of origin (also known as sources formulation or emergence).

(i) **Originated Policy.** It is that policy which is originated by the top-level managers. It therefore, flows down the level of management. The top management lays down the broad policy, which serves as the guide for the managers at lower levels of the organization. While formulating policies help delegation of authority and retain overall control.

(ii) **Appealed Policy.** Appealed is framed when a subordinate refers to an existing problem not covered by the existing policies to his superiors for policy decision. It requires immediate attention of the superiors. When the superiors make decisions, it becomes a precedent and serves as a policy for future action. Such a policy flows upward.

(iii) **Imposed Policy.** It is a policy, which is imposed by some external force like government, trade union or trade association. It is framed complying the force, which cannot be avoided. Labor policy is framed to meet the various provisions of labor laws or the terms of a collective agreement.

2. On the Basis of Function

The policy may be classified on the basis of different functional areas of the management, such as sales policy, production policy, financial policy, personnel policy, etc.

3. On the Basis of Level of Organization

I. **Top management policy.** It is framed and used by top managers, Therefore, it is known as basic policy. Such policy is applicable to whole of the organization. It includes policies relating to product selection, sales forecasting, size of the enterprise, budgeting etc.

II. **Middle-management policy.** Middle management includes area specialist's i.e. departmental heads, which take decisions and chalk out their own programmes and policies in harmony with the major policy decision of the entire organization. The specialists are invariably consulted in formulating the policies in their areas. Policies, formulated and followed by the middle management include sale policy production policy, financial policy, sales promotion policy etc.

Middle management policies may be further sub-divided into two groups:

(a) **Upper Middle management policies.** These include, policies relating to special areas, such as sales, production, finance, marketing etc. The departmental heads frames these.

(b) **Lower Middle management policies.** These are related to sub-activities within particular department i.e. sales promotion policies, advertisement policies, accounting policies, discount policies etc.

(c) **Lower Level management policy.** Lower level management includes foremen, supervisors etc., who are the heads of particular activities. The area of operation of such policy is very limited. These policies include policies regarding assignment of jobs, provision of tools, evaluation performance of his plant and labor etc.

4. On the Basis of being written or unwritten

(i) **Written policy.** Policy, which is reduced to black and white written policy. Written policy has advantage over unwritten or implied policy, because it is very clear and reveals the intention of the management. It is definite and cannot be interpreted otherwise.

(ii) **Unwritten policy.** Unwritten policy is handed down by word of mouth. It is flexible and may be adapted and adjusted to any circumstances easily. But it is not quite definite and may give rise to misgivings.

(iii) **Implied Policy.** It is neither written nor verbal. It may be inferred from the behavior of the managers and subordinates. It may change with the change of person.

7.3 Distinctions between policies and rules

1. Meaning

Policy is general statement or understanding which guides

the lower level management in decision-making. Rule on the other hand, is specific statement, which serves as guide to behavior or action.

2. Nature

Policy indicates broad area of action within which the management may exercise discretion. Rule is rather rigid. It strictly defines what should or should not be done, thus, leaving no room for discretion.

3. Formulation

Policy is generally formulated to the top and middle level. The middle level management formulates rule.

4. Relationship with time sequence

Policy includes standing answer to recurring questions. It may be interpreted and may be applied in different situations. Rule, on the other hand, is very rigid and cannot be interpreted. It may be applied only in given situations.

7.4 Distinction between Objective and Policy

1. Basic purpose

Objective is the purpose for which the organization exists. Without objective, existence of organization is aimless. Policy on the other hand, is not basic for the existence of an organization, though without policy organizational actions are bound to be less optimal.

2. Focus

Objective is the end towards which all activities of an

organization are directed. Policy provides only guidelines, which facilitate the accomplishment of predetermined objectives.

3. Philosophy

Objective reflects management philosophy. It summarizes the intention of the management in a generating; policy provides meaning and contents to objective.

4. Nature

Objective determines what is to be done in the organization. All activities are directed towards objective policy determines how the work is to be done to achieve the organizational objectives.

5. Formulation

The top management always lays down objective. Where as policy may be formulated at the top and middle management.

7.5 Distinguish between Policy and Strategy

1. Purpose

Policy is a guideline to the thinking and action of those who make decision while the strategy provides direction in which human and physical resources are deployed in order to maximize the chance of achieving objectives.

2. Timing

Policy is a guideline for making decisions in repetitive situations. Thus, policy decision is always in advance.

Strategy on the other hand, is situational. Decision may be taken only to meet the unusual, exceptional and abnormal situations.

3. Delegation

As policy provides guidelines for decision-making and implementation, it may be delegated downward in the organization. As strategy cannot be decided in advance, the question of its delegation does not arise. Thus, strategy formulation may require last minute change in the decision depending upon the situation.

4. Long term Vs Temporary

Policy is a standing plan and is formulated for a long period. Strategy is non-repetitive plan, which may need frequent changes. Hence, it is temporary arrangement.

5. Role of Competition

Policy is general not based on competitor's activities. It is formulated to guide actions for achieving the organizational objectives. Strategy, on the other hand, is generally formulated in the light of competitor's move.

7.6 Steps in Policy Formulation

1. Definition of policy Area

Identifying the area in which policies are needed is the first step in policy formulation. The objectives, needs, and environment of the organization should be kept in view in defining areas for policy formulation. There are two possible areas of policy formulation.

1. Various managerial functions, namely planning, organizing, staffing, directing and controlling.

2. Functional areas of business such as production, marketing, finance etc.

2. Analysis of facts and information

Internal and External environment of the enterprises is carefully analyzed to identify opportunities and constraints, strength and weakness etc. Internal Environment involves human and physical resources, organizational structure, workers, management relations, manpower, inventory, values etc. External Environment includes social, political, economic and technological conditions in the country.

3. Evaluation of Alternatives

Each of the policy alternatives is evaluated in terms of its contribution to objective. That policy alternative is the best, which is likely to yield the best possible results for the organization. Costs, benefits and resources required should be given due place in evaluating the policy alternatives.

4. Choice of Policy

After evaluation and making consultation with the lower levels, the most appropriate alternative, should be selected this is likely to contribute the most to the realization of organizational objectives. This is human choice of policy.

5. Putting the policy in writing

There are two reasons why policies should be put in writing. First, a policy will be vague unless it is written down. Second, if a policy is in writing, it shows what management really means.

6. Communication of policy

After the policy is written it must be communicated to those who are responsible for putting the policy into action.

7. Implementation

After the polices are adopted, they are put to action. Factors necessary for the implementation of policies such as suitable organization structure, developing and motivating people to take up work, designing effective control and information system and allocation of resources etc.

7.7 Principles of Policy Formulation or Characteristics of a Sound Policy

1. Related to objectives

A policy should be based on organization objectives. It should contribute towards the achievement of those objectives from which it is derived. It should be capable of relating objectives to functions, physical factors and company personnel. Activities, which do not contribute to objectives, should be eliminated in formulating policy.

2. Planned formulation

A policy must be the result of a careful and well thought of formulation process rather than the result of opportunistic permanent nature. Therefore ad-hocism should be avoided because it is likely to create confusion.

3. Fairly clear

Policy should be precise and comprehensive as far as possible. Precision and comprehension does not mean ambiguity. The policy should be clear enough to leave no room for misinterpretation. It must provide some discretion for managerial decisions.

4. Balance between stability as well as flexibility

A sound policy maintains a balance between stability and flexibility. Being a long-term proposition a policy should not be changed overnight. The members should be aware about what they are required to do in certain matters. But it should not be so rigid that it may not be changed when need arises. In a changed situation, the old policy becomes obsolete and needs change. It should be flexible enough to keep the organization in time with the times.

5. Consistent

The policy should provide consistency in the operation of organizational functions. Each function in the organization is related to other functions. If the policy in one area is inconsistent with another area there may be conflict resulting into inefficiency. This happens frequently in function, which is closely related such as production and marketing or finance etc. Hence, policies should be formulated in an integrated way so that policies in each area contribute to other areas also.

6. Written

Policies should be precise, clear and written as far as possible. Clearly specified policy works better than one, which is interpreted by the organization members. A written policy becomes more specific and clear and leaves no room for ambiguity or misinterpretation. Every person responsible for taking decisions may know what action he may take against the erring persons. A written policy is easier to communicate through organizational manuals.

7. Communication

Formulation of policies alone is not sufficient. Unless they are properly communicated to those who are responsible for taking decisions in the light of the policy, no meaningful purpose can be served. Hence a system should be developed to communicate policies to them. Written policies may be communicated easily. Unwritten policies require more interaction between policy formulators and policy implementers.

8. Thorough knowledge of Internal and External Factors

Policy makers should be fully aware of the internal and external factors, which may affect the implementation of policy. Policy makers should support each other. They should note their impact on employees in all departments. They should recognize all economic principles in line with laws of the land and compatible with the public interest.

9. Just, Fair and Equitable

Policies should be just, fair and equitable to both internal and external groups. For example, a recruitment policy should be such that it does not limit opportunities to bright candidates from within or outside the organization. Bright candidates should be given chance to ensure justice.

10. Reasonable

Policies must be reasonable and capable of being accomplished. Suggestions and reactions should be invited and given due weight age to make the policy acceptable to those who are affected by them.

11. Review

After a policy is formulated, the policy maker should

scrutinize it at regular intervals to find out its relevance in the wake of continuous changes in the environment. Periodic organizational review of policies is necessary to avoid organizational complacency or managerial stagnation.

7.8 Limitations of Policy Formulation

1. No Universal Solutions

Policy does not offer universal solutions to all problems. It is framed under particular situations and remains suitable under those circumstances only. As the fast changing economic, social and political situations influence the working of an enterprise, new policy is required under changed situations. This may be met by constantly evaluating a policy. Policy may be modified as per the requirements of new situations.

2. No Instant Solutions

A policy does not provide instant solutions in problems. It is only a guideline for the decision-maker. The solutions are to be found by the executives themselves. Policy cannot replace human judgment under any circumstances.

3. Dampen Human Initiations

Too many policies kill the initiative of managers. They become habituated to act according to policy and do not try to use their judgment. Policy leaves little room for individual initiative.

4. No Substitute for Human Judgment

Policy does not provide standard solutions to various problems. It is only a guideline, which helps managers in taking decisions. Managers have to judge the things according to the prevailing environment.

Review questions

Two mark questions

1. Define the term Policy?
2. Highlignt the essentials of Policy Formulation?
3. What do you mean by Imposed Policy?
4. What do you mean by Implied Policy?
5. Distinguish between Policy and Rule?
6. Highlight the differences between Objective and Policy?
7. Distinguish between Policy and Strategy
8. What are the limitations of Policy?

Part – B

1. Briefly explain the Classification of Policies?
2. Enumerate the Steps in Policy Formulation?
3. Describe how Policies are formulated?

Chapter - 8

Planning Premises

8.1 Planning Premises

Nature of Planning Premises

Planning premises provide a framework for planning a basis action, in the midst of uncertainties in the business environment. Planning premises imply not only the assumptions about the future, but also prediction. Effective planning is largely dependent upon the correct knowledge in choice of planning premises. If planning premises are changed planning will have to be modified accordingly.

Purpose of Premises

Innumerable forces and factors react upon business economy. While formulating premises a manager must consider these forces and factors. Such forces may be internal or external. It is neither necessary nor practicable for a manager to keep all these factors in mind. He must concentrate on strategic factors and forces which have material bearing his business, may ignore many subtle forces and minor factors because they affect the business to a lesser extent. The recognition of strategic, crucial and limiting factors guides the manager to select the proper and adequate premises upon which he may raise the super structure of planning. One of the major purposes of premises is to facilitate the planning process by guide directing, simplifying and reducing the degree of uncertainties in it.

8.2 Classification of Planning Premises

1. Internal and external Premises

(i) Internal Premises: These exist within a business

enterprise and include the resources and abilities of enterprise in the form of men, machines, money and methods. The most important internal premises are competence of managerial personnel and skill of labor force.

(ii) External Premises: These centre round the various type of markets i.e. the product market, the material, the money market, the labor market, and so on As the political, social and economic conditions are important determinates of market they fall under the category of external premises. Population growth, government policies and regulations, general economy and business cycles and technological change are some of the external premises which has great importance.

2. Tangible and Intangible Premises

(i) Tangible Premises: These are those which can be measured quantitatively in one way or the other such as money, time and units of production etc.

(ii) Intangible Premises: These are those, which cannot be measured quantitatively. The examples of such premises are reputation of the concern, public relations, employee morale, motivation etc. In planning, both tangible and intangible premises must be taken into account.

3. Fully Controllable, Semi-controllable and Uncontrollable Premises

(i) Fully controllable: These are factors subject to the decision of the management. For example, it is well within the jurisdiction of the management to decide what policies, procedures, rules and strategies are to be followed in the organization. The management may change them as the circumstances warrant in order to achieve the organizational objectives.

(ii) Semi-controllable Factors: Though these factors are not fully controllable, yet the management has some degree of control over them. Examples of such premises are demand of the industry's product, union-management relations etc.

(iii) Uncontrollable Premises: These are factors, which are quite uncontrollable. Therefore, they are unpredictable. However, they are important in plan formulation as they dictate the need of revising the plan in accordance with the current development. Such factors are war, natural calamities, new discoveries and inventions, emergency legislations and other like events, which cannot be predicted and controlled. All intangible premises such as human behavior cannot be predicted with accuracy.

4. Constant and Variable Premises

(i) Constant premises: These are those, which behave, in the similar fashion, irrespective of action taken. They are definite, known and well understood. As the behavior of constant premises is not subject to change, these are ignored in planning. Such factors are men, machine and money.

(ii) Variable premises: They are those which vary in relation to the course of action taken. These factors have a significant bearing on the success of the plan. While formulating plans the management must encompass all possible variable factors. As their variations are dependent upon the action taken by the management, these cannot be controlled and predicted. Sales volume of the enterprise can be partly controlled by the management. Certain other factors affect the sales volume of the enterprise but are quite uncontrollable. Managers can only peer into the future to study their variations in the years to come. Forecasting about them gives the manager an idea or knowledge of their variations. But is case of constant variable live casting is not required.

5. Foreseeable and Unforeseeable Premises

(i) **Foreseeable Premises:** These are those, which are definite and well-known and can be foreseen with certainly. All constant premises are foreseeable premises.

(ii) **Unforeseeable Premises:** These are those which are uncontrollable hence unpredictable. Examples such as war, strike, natural calamities etc.

Review questions

Two mark questions

1. What do you mean by Internal and External Premises?
2. What is the Purpose of Premises?
3. What do you mean by Tangible and Intangible Premises?
4. What is Constant and Variable Premises?
5. What is Foreseeable and Unforeseeable premises

Part – B

1. What are the Planning Premises? Explain the Classification of Planning Premises?

Chapter - 9

Decision Making

9.1 Decision Making

Definitions

George R. Terry, "Decision-making is the selection based on some criteria from two or more possible alternatives."

John McDonald, "The business executive is by profession a decision-maker, uncertainty is his opponent, overcoming it is his mission. Whether the outcome is a consequence of luck or wisdom, the moment of decision-making is without doubt the most creative event in the life of the executive."

D.E. Mc Farland, "A decision is an act of choice wherein an executive forms a conclusion about what must be done in a given situation. A decision represents a behavior chosen from a number of possible alternatives."

Henry Sisk and Clifston Williams, "A decision is the selection of a course of action from two or more alternatives; the decision making process is a sequence of steps leading to that selection."

Shull et.al, "Decision-making is a conscious and human process, involving both individual and social phenomenon based upon factual and value premises, which concludes with a choice of one behavioral activity from among one or more alternatives with the intention of moving towards some desired state of affairs."

Mary Cushing Nites, "Decision-making takes place in

adopting the objectives and choosing the means and again when a change in the situation creates a necessity for adjustments."

R.S. Davar, "Decision-making may be defined as the selection based on some criteria of one behavior alternative from two or more possible alternatives."

9.2 Characteristics of Decision-Making

1. Decision-making is a selection process. The best alternative is selected out of many available alternatives. If there is only one alternative, there is no decision-making.
2. Decision-making is the end process. Decision-making is preceded by detailed discussion and selection of alternatives.
3. Decision-making is the application of intellectual abilities to a great extent. An intelligent man alone can take a good decision.
4. Decision gives happiness to an endeavor who takes various steps to collect all the information which is likely to affect a decision.
5. Decision-making is a dynamic process. An individual takes a number of decisions each day.
6. Decision-making is situational. An individual takes decision according to the situations prevailing. Different decisions may be taken to solve the same problem. The reason is that the situation is changed from time to time.
7. Decision is taken to achieve the objectives of an organization.

8. Decision-maker has the freedom to take a decision, which involves the using of resources in specified ways.

9. A decision may be both positive and negative.

9.3 Steps in Decision - Making Process

Decision-making is the process through which managers identify organizational problems and attempt to resolve them.

Decision-making is the process of selecting and implementing alternatives consistent with a goal. It is a series of activities that begins with defining the purpose or goal of the decision and involves developing and evaluating alternatives, selecting and implementing the alternative. Also monitoring the results to ensure that the decision goals are achieved. This entire process, from setting the decision goal to making sure the goal has been achieved is called decision – making

Steps in decision making process

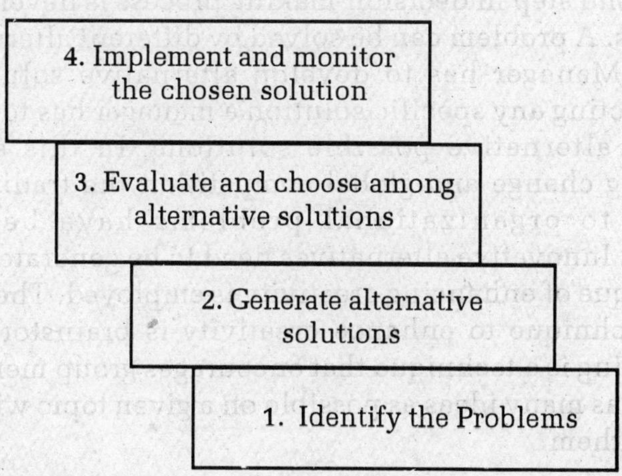

Decisions are taken for future actions. Hence decision-making is a risky and challenging task for a manager. Managers may not always make the right decision, but they can use their knowledge of appropriate decision-making processes. Manager's performance is judged on his decision-making capability.

1. Identify the Problem

The first step in the decision making process is identifying the problem. Problem cannot be identified without a search. Organizational problems are the difference between expected results and actual situation. Identifying the problem involves three main activities.

1. **Scanning:** Monitoring the work condition for changing circumstances that can indicate the emergence of problem.
2. **Categorize:** Attempts to categorize the situation as a problem or non-problem.
3. **Diagnose:** Gathering additional information and diagnose the problem's nature and causes.

2. Generate Alternative Solutions

The second step in decision-making process is developing alternatives. A problem can be solved by different alternative solutions. Manager has to develop alternative solutions. Before selecting any specific solution a manager has to think on all the alternative possible solutions. In this era of accelerating change and global competition the traditional solutions to organizational problems have become ineffective. Innovative alternatives need to be generated. For this technique of enhancing creativity is employed. The most familiar technique to enhance creativity is brainstorming. Brainstorming is a technique that encourages group members to generate as many ideas as possible on a given topic without evaluating them.

3. Evaluating and Choosing an Alternative

When all the possible and realistic alternatives have been identified, the focus of decision-process shifts to evaluating those alternatives, to identifying the strengths and weaknesses of each option. Each alternative should be evaluated systematically according to general criteria's like feasibility, quality, acceptability, costs, ethics etc.

Feasibility refers to the extent to which an alternative can be accomplished with given related organizational constraints e.g. time, technology, and budget.

Quality refers to how effectively an alternative solves the problem under consideration.

Acceptability is the degree to which concerned people will be affected by implementing the alternative and people willing to support alternative.

Costs are the monetary expenditures and other resources required to implement any alternative.

Ethics refers to the compatibility of an alternative with the social and moral responsibility.

Either quantitative or qualitative approaches can be used to evaluate and choose an alternative. **Quantitative approach** uses mathematical and statistical techniques to analyze the decision alternatives. Quantitative approaches are linear programming, Break-even Analysis, Decision tree analysis. **Qualitative approach** uses comparison of characteristics of alternatives and takes relevant decision. A typical qualitative approach is T-chart.

4. Implement and Monitor the Chosen Solution

A decision is just a choice until it is implemented and

monitored. Implementation of decision reveals its effectiveness and significance in achieving the desired goals.

Successful implementation usually depends on careful planning and sensitivity to those involved in the implementation or affected by it.

Even effective implementation does not complete the action phase of the decision-making process. Once it is implemented, the decision must be monitored to ensure that the alternative put into action is moving the organization closer to its goals. It is only the monitoring phase that confirms that the organizations goals have been achieved

Steps and Activities in Decision-Making

The steps in; decision-making process and important activities associated with it are shown in the below table.

S.No	Steps	Activities
1.	Identify the problem	Scan the environment for changing circumstances. Categorize the situations. Diagnose the problem and the causes.
2.	Generate the alternative solution	Search the innovative ideas and alternatives
3.	Evaluate and choose an alternative	Evaluate feasibility, quality, acceptability, costs and ethics by quantitative or qualitative approach.
4.	Implement and monitor the chosen solution	Implement the solution. Monitor its effectiveness. Measure goal achievement.

Factors Affecting the Rational Decision-Making

Following factors affect the rational decision-making of managers

1. Inadequate Information

Decision-makers may have inadequate information about the problem, possible alternatives and their strengths and limitations.

2. Times and Cost

Time and cost are the limiting constraints throughout the decision-making process.

3. Perception of Decision-maker

Decision-maker's perception in identifying the problem, selecting alternative may ignore the actual critical problem.

4. Experience of Decision-maker

If decisions are to be taken with less information then extensive experience with situation becomes the key input. The experience level of the decision maker becomes the key factor.

5. Decision-maker's Personality

The perfectionist decision-maker may postpone taking decision, preferring to seek the ideal alternative. The impulsive decision maker might hurry through the decision process thinking that just to finish it at the earliest. Such personalities give negative effect of decision-maker.

6. Values of Decision-maker

A decision-maker must not reflect his own personal values rather than company's need or the personal values must not influence both the goals and the results of decision process.

7. Capacity of Decision-maker

Even after gathering perfect information it is the intelligence and calculating capacity of manager, which limits the success of any plan or decision.

9.4 Principles of Decision-Making

The manager may take a quality decision if he adopts certain principles. These principles are discussed below

1. Marginal theory of decision-making

Many economists have suggested marginal theory of decision-making. They believe that a business has started to earn profits. A manager must take a decision, which results in maximizing the profits. Therefore, economists argue that the very purpose of an organization is aimed at maximizing profits.

Decision-making should be based on marginal analysis. Here, the manager adopts the Principle of Law of Diminishing Returns. If the management appoints additional labor and uses additional capital, the production may be increased proportionately at reduced rates. A time comes when there is no increase in production with the appointment of additional labor and using additional capital. Then, the appointment of additional labor and using of additional capital will be stopped. In this way, the production of the last unit is marginal. Thus, this marginal principle is applied while taking decisions relating to sales, advertisement, promotion, training and the like.

2. Mathematical theory

Venture analysis, game theory, probability theory and waiting theory are some of the mathematical theories. A manager takes a decision on the basis of mathematical theory. Mathematical theory gives scientific approach to the manager while taking a decision.

3. Psychological theory

A manager takes a decision on the basis of his aspiration, technological skill, personality, social status and organization status. Though the manager is expected to take a decision confined to the scope of his responsibility and authority, there is an impact of psychology over the decision. The reason is that decision-making is a mental process.

4. Principle of alternatives

If there is only one alternative to solve a problem, there is no need of taking a decision. Decision is a selection process all the alternatives are evaluated and screened in the order of their usefulness. Finally, the best alternative is selected according to the circumstances and purpose.

5. Principle of limiting factors

The fundamentals of a problem are studied. An inference or a conclusion is drawn on the basis of study. The manager takes a decision with the help of conclusion or inference. The decision may be based on a limiting factor. The limiting factor may be time, cost or resources. Decisions are supposed to be good and the limiting factor is considered while taking a decision. The reason is that this decision can be implemented in a particular situation.

6. Principle of participation

This principle is based on human behavior and human - relationship. Each and every person wants to be treated' as an important person. So, the management may allow the employees to have a say in the process of decision-making.

9.5 Types of Decisions

1. Programmed decisions

They are otherwise called routine decisions or structured decisions. The reason is that these types of decisions are taken frequently and they are repetitive in nature. This decision is taken within the purview of the policy of the organization. Only lower level management take programmed decision and has short-term impact. Granting over timework, placing purchase order (for materials) etc., are some of the examples of programmed decisions. There is a clear-cut procedure to take programmed decisions. The decision-maker need not ask anything from the Personnel Manager or Board of Directors while taking programmed decisions.

2. Non-programmed decisions

They are otherwise called strategic decisions or basic decisions or policy decisions or unstructured decisions. Top management people take this decision whenever the need arises. The management before taking a policy decision makes a careful analysis. The management may publish its policy in small book, which is known as policy manual. Policy decision involves heavy expenditure to management. Starting a new business, whether to export or not, acquisition of a business etc. are some of the examples of nonprogrammed decisions. This decision has a long-term impact on business. A slight mistake in the policy decision is bound to injure the entire organization.

3. Major decision

Major decision relates to the purchase of fixed assets with more value. The purchase of land and building is an example of major decision. This decision is taken- by the top management.

4. Minor decision

Minor decision relates to the purchase of current assets with less value. Purchase of pencil, pen, ink, etc. is some of the examples of minor decision. Lower level management people take this decision.

5. Operative decision

A decision, which relates to day-to-day operation of an organization, is known as operative decision. Middle level management people take this type of decision normally. The reason is that they are working at supervisory level and have a good knowledge of the operations. Middle level management people fix the time of payment of overtime wages. It is an example of operative decision.

6. Organizational decision

The decision-maker takes a decision and implements it for effective functioning of organization and it is called organizational decision. He takes this decision on his authority and capacity.

7. Personal decision

The decision-maker takes a decision for his personal life, which is known as personal decision. He implements this decision in his home and sets right his personal life. This decision does not reflect the functioning of an organization.

The decision-maker is not a member of an organization while taking a personal decision.

8. Individual decision

Confusion exists in the difference between individual decision and personal decisions. They are not one and the same. The decision-maker is a member of an organization while taking an individual decision. He can implement it in the organization. He is delegated with authority to take individual decision. He considers the policy and situation prevailing in an organization while taking individual decision.

9. Group decision

The top management forms a committee for specific purposes. Here, the top management feels that no individual can take effective decision to solve a problem. The top management fixes the time within which the committee is expected to submit its report with concrete decisions.

10. Departmental decision

Here, the decision-maker is department head or department manager. He takes a decision to run the department. Department decision has no impact on other departments. This decision is implemented within the concerned department itself.

11. Non-economic decision

Non-economic decision refers to a decision, which does not incur any expenses. These types of decisions are taken at all levels of management. A decision, which relates to setting right the moral behavior of workers, is termed as non-economic decision.

12. Crisis decision

A decision is taken to meet unexpected situations. There is no possibility and time for the decision-maker for getting through investigation while taking a crisis decision. It may be otherwise called spot decision. The reason is that whenever a need arises, the decision maker has to take a decision without wasting a second.

13. Research decision

A decision is taken after analyzing the pros and cons of a particular matter. There is no pressure on the decision-maker to take such a decision. Research decision requires a lot of information. The quality of research decision is fully depending upon the availability of reliable information.

14. Problem decision

A decision is taken to solve a problem. The problem may be an expected one or an unexpected one. Besides, the arrived decision does not create any more problems to the organization.

15. Opportunity decision

This pertains to a decision taken to make use of the advantages available to the company or organization. The advantages may be increasing the turnover, introducing a new product, building of another similar unit to avoid competition etc.

16. Certainty decision

Here, the term certainty refers to accurate knowledge of the outcome from each choice. For example, introducing a new product or increasing the selling price and the like will
8 maximize ascertaining how much profits. There is only one

outcome for each choice. The decision-maker himself knows the outcome and consequences of choice.

17. Uncertainty decision

The outcome is not accurate or several outcomes are possible whenever a decision is taken. The reason is that the decision-maker has incomplete knowledge and he does not know the consequences. For example, while marketing a new product, the decision (amount of profits) depends upon the prosperity period of that product. If the prosperity period is long, the amount of profit is high and vice versa.

Management people take a number of decisions everyday. These decisions are aimed at solving the existing problems. No decision creates any new problem to the management. There should be justice in taking a decision.

Review Questions

Two mark questions

1. Define Decision- Making?
2. Highlight the Characteristics of Decision – Making?
3. What is Quantitative Approach?
4. What is Qualitative Approach?

Part – B

1. Briefly explain the steps in Decision – Making Process?
2. Briefly explain the principles of Decision - Making?
3. Explain a few Types of Decision with an example?

Chapter - 10

Organizing

10.1 Introduction

The word organization is derived from the word "organism" which means an organized body with connected interdependent parts sharing common life. Organization is a mechanism or structure, which helps the activities to be performed effectively. The organization is established for the purpose of achieving the business objectives. The business objectives may differ from one business to another. Organization can be compared to a human body. The human body consists of hands, feet, eyes, ears, mouth and etc. These parts are performing their work independently and at the same time, one part cannot be a substitute to another. The same principles can be identified in the organization also. The organization consists of different department. Each department performs its work independently and cannot be a substitute to another.

10.2 Definitions

Mc Farland

"An identified group of people contributing their efforts towards the attainment of goals is called an organization.

Allen

"The process of identifying and grouping the work is to be performed, defining and delegating responsibility and authority and establishing relationships for the purpose of enabling people to work most effectively together in accomplishing objective".

Mooney and Reily

"Organization is the form of every human association for the attainment of a common purpose."

Chester Bernard

"A system of co-operative activities of two or more persons is called organization".

Meaning

Organization is the detailed arrangement of work and working conditions in order to perform the assigned activities in an effective manner.

10.3 Formal Vs Informal Organization

S.No	Key factor	Formal	Informal
1.	Origin	Created consciously and deliberately.	Created because of psychological forces existing at the work place.
2.	Purpose	Legitimate objectives of the organization	Created for personal special-psychological satisfaction
3.	Size	May be quite large in size	Always small in size in order to maintain group cohesiveness.

4.	Number of sub groups	Many sub groups in a single organization Ex. Departments	Many informal groups. But individual may be numbers of many informal groups
5.	Authority	Membership derive authority through formal delegation	People give authority to leaders because they derive the maximum benefits.
6.	Nature of organization	Stable; exist for a long period, membership is specified through organizational process.	Quite unstable in nature, formation and functioning depends upon the value systems and general liking and deriving and of the personality is features of the members concerned.
7.	Behavior of members	Behaviors is governed by formal rules and regulations	Behavior is generated by norms, beliefs and values of groups.
8.	Communication	All communication in the formal groups are expected to pass through specified channels in both oral and written	The communication pass through informal oral channel only.
9.	Abolition	The management has the authority to abolish the formal organization.	The management cannot abolish the informal organization
10.	Types of relationship	Legitimate	Personal and Social relationship

10.4 Principles of Organization

The work can be completed in time whenever a technique or a principle is adopted. So, the success or failure of an organization depends upon the principles to be followed in the organization. The principles of organization may be termed as a tool used by the organization. Some experts like Taylor, Fayol and Urwick have given the principles of organization. They are briefly discussed below

1. Principle of definition

It is necessary to define and fix the duties, responsibilities and authority of each worker. In addition to that the organizational relationship of each worker with others should be clearly defined in the organizational set up.

2. Principle of objective

The activities at all levels of organization structure should be geared to achieve the main objectives of the organization. The activities of the different departments or sections may be different in nature and in approach, but these should be concentrated only for achieving the main objectives.

3. Principle of specialization or division of work

Division of work means that the entire activities of the organization are suitably grouped into departments or sections. The departments or sections may be further divided into several such units so as to ensure maximum efficiency. This will help to fix up the right man to the right job and reduce waste of time and resources.

The work is assigned to each person according to his educational qualification, experience, skill and interests. He should be mentally and physically fit for performing the work assigned to him. The required training may be provided to the needy persons. It will result in attaining specialization in a particular work or area.

4. Principle of co-ordination

The objectives of the organization may be achieved quickly whenever co-ordination exists among the workers. At the same time each work can be done effectively by having co-ordination. The final objective of all organizations is to get smooth and effective co-ordination.

5. Principle of authority

When many persons are working together in one place, there will be a difference of power and authority. Of these persons, some will rule and others will be ruled. Normally, maximum powers are vested with the top executives of the organization. These senior members should delegate their authorities to their subordinates on the basis of their ability. In certain cases, the subordinates are motivated through the delegation of authority and they perform the work efficiently with responsibility.

6. Principle of responsibility

Each person is responsible for the work completed by him. Authority is delegated from the top level to the bottom level of the organization. But the responsibility can be delegated to some extent. While delegating the authority, there is no need of delegation of responsibility. So, the, responsibility of the junior staff members should be clearly defined.

7. Principle of explanation

While allocating duties to the persons, the extent of liabilities of the person would be clearly explained to the concerned person. It will enable the person to accept the authority and discharge his duties.

8. Principle of efficiency

Each work can be completed efficiently wherever the climate or the organizational structure facilitates the completion of work. The work should be completed with minimum members, in less time, with minimum resources and within the right time.

9. Principle of uniformity

The organization should make the work distribution in such a manner that there should be an equal status and equal authority and powers among the same line officers. It will avoid the problems of dual subordination or conflicts in the organizational set up. Besides, it increases co-ordination among the officers.

10. Principle of correspondence

Authority and responsibility should be in parity with each other. If it is not so, the work cannot be effectively discharged by any officers, whatever his ability may be. At the same time, if authority alone is delegated without responsibility, the authority may be misused. In another sense, if responsibility is delegated without the authority, it is a dangerous one.

11. Principle of unity of command

This is also sometimes called the principle of responsibility. The organizational set up should be arranged in such a way that a subordinate should receive the instruction or direction from one authority or boss. If there is no unity of command in any organizational set up, the subordinate may neglect his duties. It will result in the non-completion of any work. In the absence of unity of command, there is no guidance available to the subordinates and there is no controlling power for the top executives of the organization. Further, some subordinates will have to do more work and some others will not do any work at all.

12. Principle of balance

There are several units functioning separately under one organizational set up. The work of one unit might have been commenced after the completion of the work by another unit. So, it is essential that the sequence of work should be arranged scientifically.

13. Principle of equilibrium balance

The expansions of business activities require some changes in the organization. In certain periods, some sections or departments are overloaded and some departments are under loaded. During this period, due weightage should be given on the basis of the new workload. The overloaded sections or departments can be further divided into sub sections or sub-departments. It would entail in the effective control over all the organizational activities.

14. Principle of continuity

It is essential that there should be a re-operation of objectives, re-adjustment of plants and provision of opportunities for the development of future management. This process is taken over by every organization periodically.

15. Principle of span of control

This is also called span of management or span of supervision or levels of organization. This principle is based on the principle of relationship.

Span of control refers to the maximum number of members effectively supervised by a single individual. The number of members may be increased or decreased according to the nature of work done by the subordinate or the ability of the supervisor. In the administration area, under one executive, nearly four or five subordinates may work. In the lower level or the factory level, under one supervision, the twenty or twenty-five number of workers may work. The span of control enables the smooth functioning of the organization.

16. Principle of leadership facilitation

The organizational set up may be arranged in such a way that the persons with leadership qualities are appointed in key positions. The leadership qualities are honesty, devotion, enthusiasm and inspiration.

17. Principle of exception

The seniors disturb the junior officers only when the work is not done according to the plans laid down. It automatically reduces the work of middle level officers and top-level officers. So, the top-level officers may use the time gained by reduction in workload for framing the policies and chalking out the plans of organization.

18. Principle of flexibility

The organizational set up should be flexible to adjust to the changing environment of business. The organization should avoid the complicated procedures and permit an expansion or contraction of business activities.

19. The scalar principle

This is also called chain of command or line of authority. Normally, the line of authority flows from the top level to bottom level. It also establishes the line of communication. Each and every person should know who is his superior and to whom he is answerable.

20. Principle of simplicity and homogeneity

The organization structure should be simple. It is necessary to understand a person who is working in the same organization. If the organization structure becomes a complex one, junior officers do not understand the level and the extent of responsibility for a particular activity. The simplicity of the organizational structure enables the staff members to maintain equality and homogeneity. If equality and homogeneity are maintained in one organization, it is possible to determine whether the staff members discharge their duties to realize the objective of the organization.

21. Principle of Unity of Direction

This is also called the principle of co-ordination. The major plan is divided into sub-plans in a good organizational set up. A particular group or department takes up each sub-plan. All the groups or departments are requested to co-operate to attain the main objectives or in implementing major plan of the organization.

22. Principle of joint decisions

In the business organization, there are number of decisions taken by the officers to run the business. If a complicated problem arises more than one member examines the problems and takes the decisions. Whenever the decision is taken jointly, the decision gives the benefit for a long period and the decision is based on various aspects of the organizational set up.

10.5 Nature and Purpose of Organization

Organization is the pioneering step of the management. The functions of management are sitting over the strong organizational set up. A palace may be constructed only when a very strong foundation is laid. The same principle is followed here. Organization is the foundation of management. Without organization, the functions of management such as planning, organizing, staffing, directing, coordinating and controlling cannot succeed. Organization supplies the human and material resources and helps to achieve the objectives of business. The organization provides the means or techniques with strong efforts for more production and effective completion of the work. Organization increases the certainty and promptness in the completion of work by assigning fixed duties to every person. Whenever the duties are fixed, it automatically develops team spirit towards the realization of common goals. Initially, the total work of the enterprise can be divided into various parts and then linked with all the parts as and when the need arises to achieve main objectives. The connection of various parts of the organization is given by the authority relationship of organizational structure. The relationship may operate upward, downward, and sidewise of the organization.

1. Division of labor

The total work can be divided into many parts for effective performance of the work. One person or a group of persons may complete each part of work. But, all the parts of the work are done with the aim to achieve the main objective of the organization. The work is assigned to a person who is specialized in that particular work.

If there is a proper division of labor, no person will be allowed to do anything according to his own way unless and otherwise he is not well equipped. The division of labor results in the creation of specialized persons because a person does the same work again and again. No waste of time, energy and resources are some of the advantages of division of labor. In addition to this, the division of labor results in the increase of quality output and quantity of product without any additional capital.

2. Co-ordination

Different persons are assigned to different works in one organization. But, all the works are performed to achieve the objectives. It implies that there is a need of co-ordination among the workers in an organization. Each and. every department or section of the organization should have relationship with each other, to get mutual co-operation.

3. Objectives

The objectives of the organization should be defined clearly. The objectives cannot be achieved without the existence of a good organizational structure. In turn, the organization cannot exist without objectives for a long period.

4. Authority-responsibility structure

An organization means an arrangement of position of executives by adopting a rank system. In other words, a subordinate has one boss and a superior has control over the subordinate specifically. The position of each of the executives is defined with regard to the extent of authority and responsibility vested in him to discharge the duties.

5. Communication

Every organization has its own communication system and the methods. The success of management depends upon the effective system of communication. The reason is that each and every person working in an organization should know the techniques of communication and the importance of communication. The channels of communication may be divided into formal, informal, downward and upward or horizontal.

Review questions

Two mark questions

1. What do you mean by Formal and Informal organization?
2. What do you mean by

   a) Span of control

   b) Scalar principle

   c) Principle of exception

   d) Division of work

   e) Flexibility.

Part – B

1. Distinguish between Formal and Informal Organization?
2. Briefly Explain the Principles of Organization?

Chapter - 11

Departmentation

11.1 Departmentation

Definitions

Koontz and O'Donnell

A departmentation is a process of dividing the large monolithic functional organization into small and flexible administrative units.

Departmentation is the process by which similar activities of the business are grouped into units for the purpose of facilitating smooth administration at all levels.

Meaning

It refers to the classification of activities on operations of an undertaking into functionalized categories.

Process of Departmentation

1. Identification of work
2. Analysis of details of each work
3. Description of the function of the organization
4. Entrusting the functions to a separate person who has specialized in the respective field and providing him with suitable staff.
5. Fixing the scope of authority and responsibility of the departmental heads.

11.2 Basis (OR) Types of Departmentation

There are certain basic methods of dividing the duties and responsibilities within an organizational structure. They are given below:

1. Departmentation by functions.
2. Departmentation by product or service.
3. Departmentation by regions (area or location) or territory.
4. Departmentation by customers.
5. Departmentation by process.
6. Departmentation by time.
7. Departmentation by numbers.
8. Departmentation by marketing channels.

1. Departmentation by Functions

The most commonly followed basis of departmentation is by functions. Under this departmentation, the activities are grouped on the basis of functions, which are to be performed. The following chart may help to understand the departmentation by functions:

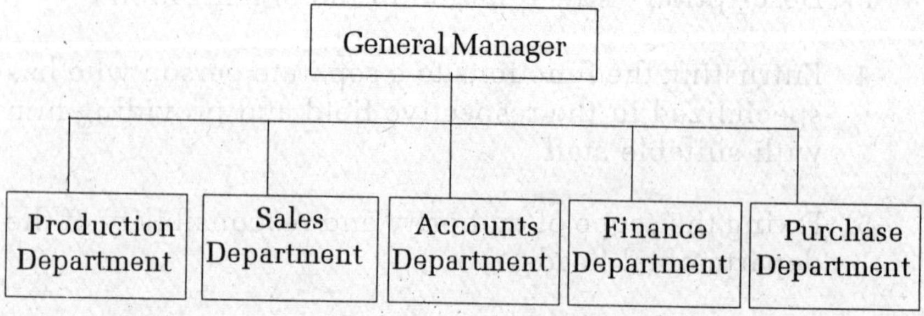

Each department is headed by one responsible person, who is directly responsible to the General Manager, According to George R. Terry, "the functions or 'activities are the pivot around which effective executives develop effective and efficient organization".

Advantages

1. It is a scientific and time-tested method.
2. It follows the principles of specialization and division of labor.
3. It ensures proper performance control.
4. It preserves the importance of each of the activities of an organization.
5. It avoids the interruptions of subsidiary groups in the primary activities.
6. Due weightage and prestige are given to the departmental managers and they are respected by top management people.
7. It facilitates co-ordination activity within the department itself and the Organization as a whole.
8. It is economical, simple and easy to understand.
9. It helps the utilization of manpower and other natural resources of the Organization.

Disadvantages

1. It makes the management control work more difficult.

2. The department heads consider themselves to be autonomous sections of the Organization. The managers will not look upon the undertaking as a unit.

3. It increases the work load and responsibility of departmental managers.

4. It doesn't offer any scope for training for the overall development of managers.

5. The departmental managers are experts in handling the problems in their departments alone. They may not be able to understand the problems of other departments.

2. Departmentation by Product or Service

This type of departmentation is made by the large-scale business unit. A single business unit may manufacture and sell different types of products. Then, each type of product or service is allocated to a separate department. Functionalized units for each product are created within the general structure of the organization. Manufacturing, sales, finance and personnel functions are arranged separately for each type of product. Each department is responsible for manufacturing a product and selling it to customers. Grouping of all activities are planned in advance within each product section. The co-ordination function is performed by the top management.

'A' Product Manager

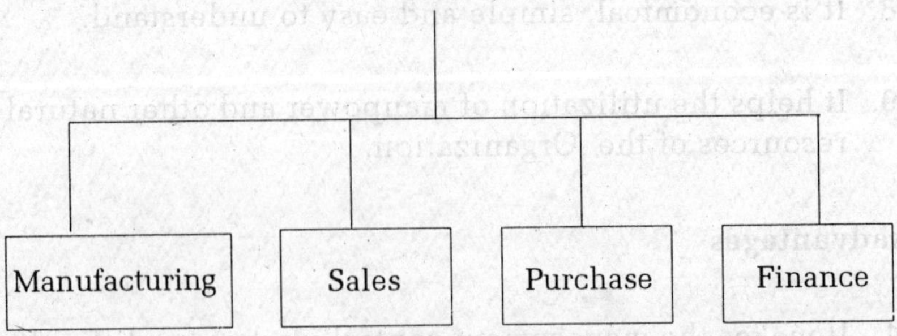

Advantages

1. Product departmentation helps in the maximum utilization of personal efficiency of workers in the area. of manufacturing and marketing of product.

2. There is a possibility of gaining economy in manufacturing and marketing of products on account of large-scale operation.

3. Better services may be provided to the customer.

4. The management knows the profitability of each product. So, it is easy to fix the responsibility on the departmental heads.

5. Proper attention may be devoted to the manufacture of a product.

6. Managers perform all the functions pertaining to the manufacture of a particular product. Then, there is the possibility of an effective co- ordination and control.

7. A new line of product can be introduced without any difficulty.

Disadvantages

1. There is a danger of duplication of work.

2. It increases the number of personnel which in turn increases the cost of operation.

3. It requires additional cost for maintaining a sales force for each type of product.

4. In proportion to the increase in the number of employees, the problem of control at the executive levels become more difficult.

5. Machines and equipments in each product department may not be used fully.

3. Departmentation by Region or Area

This method of departmentation may be suitable for a business unit which is wholly dispersed. The business activities are grouped in area-wise and each area is in charge of a single person. The local persons are appointed as salesmen in each area. It will help the business unit to increase the sales. The reason that the local person is familiar with the local language the culture and preferences of the customers.

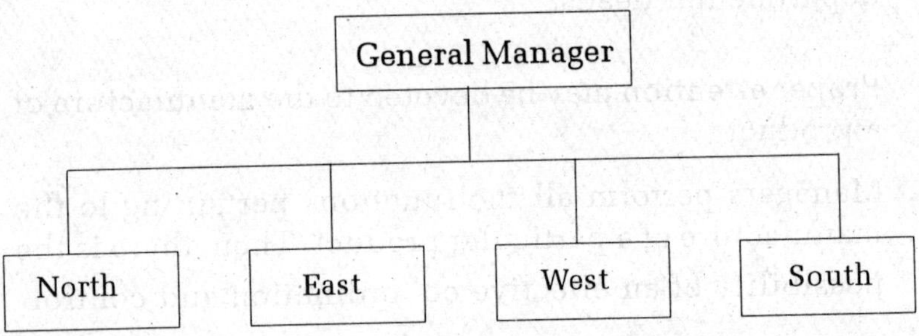

Advantages

1. It makes possible an effective span of control
2. The sales may be increased with the help of intimate knowledge about the tastes and preferences of the customers in the local market.
3. Regional managers could win the confidence of customers and remove the competitors from the market.
4. Accounts are prepared area-wise. So, the profitability of each area is known to the management.
5. It provides opportunities to managers to improve their skill in various fields.

6. This type of departmentation is more suitable for a large scale business unit.

7. Control process is very easy to manage.

Disadvantages

1. It increases the number of personnel and involves high cost of operation.

2. The control of head office is a less effective one.

3. It may also involve duplication of work.

4. A small business concern cannot manage the high cost of operation.

4. Departmentation by Customers

This type of departmentation is preferred when the various needs of customers are different in nature. For example, a bank or a financial institution may divide its loan section into number of heads and assign them to various departments, such as loans to businessmen, farmers, professionals and so on. Similarly, the sales department of a business concern could be divided into industrial goods and consumer goods. The consumable goods could again be sub-divided into perishable and non-perishable in nature.

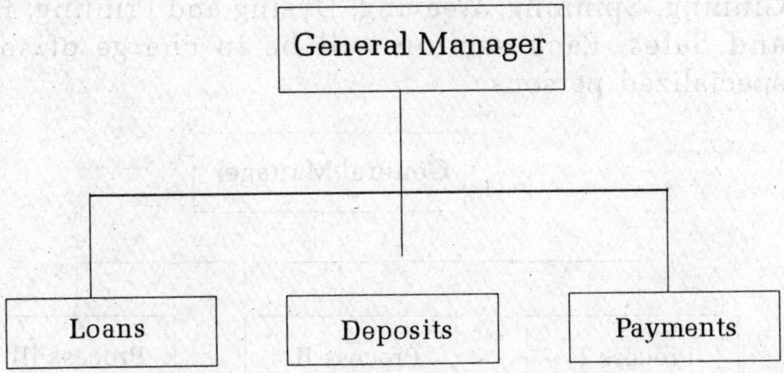

Advantages

1. It fulfils the expectations and needs of customers.
2. It develops specialization among the organizational staff.
3. Customer can dispense with the out of fashion products through the departmentation. The reason is that the business unit has intimate knowledge of the customer's tastes and preferences.
4. Each section of the customer is able to get better service from the company and helps the company to win thr goodwill, of its customers.

Disadvantages

1. There may be duplication of activities.
2. The achievement of co-ordination is very difficult.
3. There is wastage of available resources and facilities.

5. Departmentation by Process

This type of Departmentation is followed when the production activities are carried on in many places. For example, a textile mill has many departments such as Ginning, Spinning, Weaving, Dyeing and Printing, Packing and Sales. Each section will be in charge of separate specialized persons.

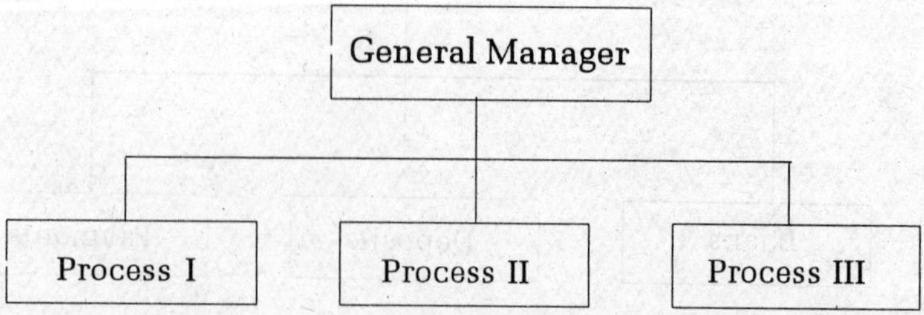

Advantages

1. The costlier machines can be used effectively.
2. There is no interruption of the departments or process in other production processes. The requirement and renewals of any process cannot affect the production of other processes.
3. There may be economy in operation.
4. There is no duplication of activities.
5. The principle of specialization and division of labor is followed.
6. This departmentation helps the top management to have effective performance control.
7. This type of departmentation is more suitable to any business unit, which manufactures a product passing through a number of processes.

Disadvantages

1. Separate rooms for operation and other facilities should be given to all the process. This results in heavy cost of operation.
2. More specialists are essential to each process.
3. It does not give good training to staff members and there is a lack of overall development of the managerial talents.

6. Departmentation by Time

The business activities are grouped together on the basis

of the time of the performance. If the work is not completed within the normal working hours, extra time will be given to complete it after the normal working hours. Only interested persons are requested to do the job and one person is responsible to supervise them. Whatever be the work performed after the normal working hours, a separate department will be in charge of this type of activity. This type of departmentation is known as departmentation by time.

•

7. Departmentation by Numbers

Small groups perform similar type of duties. A supervisor or an executive controls each group. For example, in the Army, soldiers are grouped into squads, battalions, companies, brigades and regiments on the basis of allotment of men to each unit. The principles of management span of control or span of supervision is used under this type of departmentation

8. Departmentation by Marketing Channels

This type of departmentation is adopted on the basis of the channel of distribution chosen by the particular business unit. Normally the channel of distribution is selected by the business unit on the basis of nature of goods and marketability of the product. This method of departmentation has grown in importance as business has become increasingly market-oriented.

Review questions

Two mark question

1. Define Departmentation?

2. What are the types of Departmentation?

3. What do you means Departmentation by

   (a) Function (b) Product

   (c) customer (d) process

Part- B

1. Briefly explain the types, merits and limitation of any three Departmentation of your own choice with a heat diagram?

2. Describe the Various Kinds of Departmentation?

Chapter - 12

Line Organization

12.1 Line Organization

Line organization is the simple and oldest type of organization. Under this, each department is generally a complete self-contained unit. A separate person will look after the activities of the department and he has full control over the department. This type of organization is followed in the army on the same pattern. So, it is called military organization. Under this type of organization, the line of authority flows from the top to bottom vertically. So, it is called line organization. Line organization is also called as military or scalar organization.

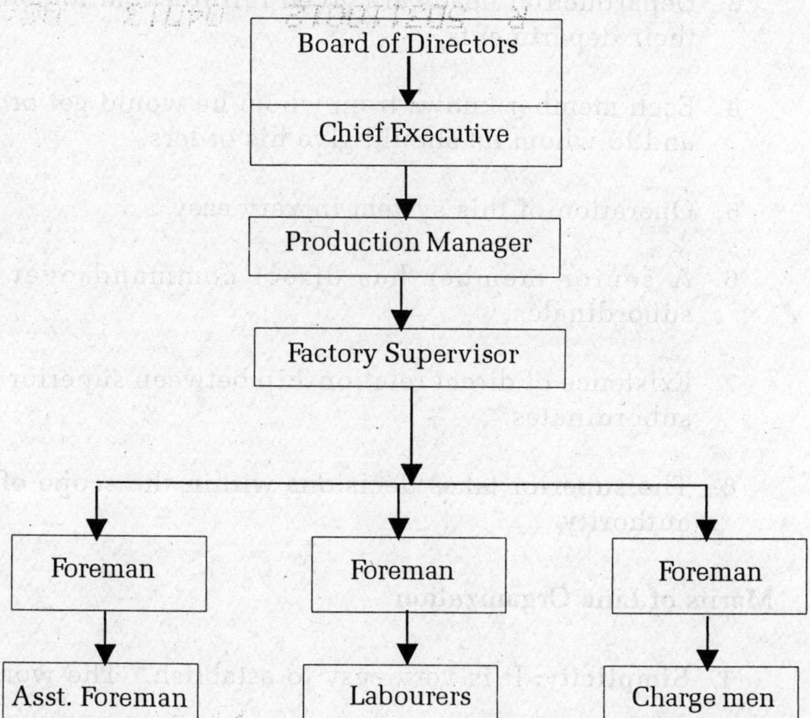

Kinds of line organization

1. **Pure line organization** – All the individuals perform the same type of work. i.e. all the workers may be engaged in a similar activity.

2. **Departmental line organization** – There is a Chief Executive at the top, under him, there are number of departments each headed by a departmental manager. Even within a department, there may be several sub-departments or units carrying different task.

The characteristics of line organization are

1. It consists of direct vertical relationships.

2. Authority flows from top level to bottom level.

3. Departmental heads are given full freedom to control their departments.

4. Each member knows from whom he would get orders and to whom he should give his orders.

5. Operation of this system in very easy.

6. A senior member has direct command over his subordinates.

7. Existence of direct relationship between superior and subordinates.

8. The superior takes decisions within the scope of his authority.

Merits of Line Organization

1. **Simplicity:** It is very easy to establish. The workers

can understand the concept and relationship with others without any difficulty.

2. **Division of authority and responsibility:** Each person has his area of authority, which is clearly explained to him. So he knows to whom he is responsible for doing the job.

3. **Unity of Control:** An individual can receive orders only from one superior. It means that a subordinate is responsible only to one superior and he gets orders only from him.

4. **Speedy action:** There is a proper division of authority and responsibility and unity of command. Hence, an individual can take decisions and execute the plans without any delay.

5. **Discipline** – The authority flows from top to bottom. Loyalty and discipline can be maintained among the employees of the organization without much difficulty.

6. **Economical:** It is a single type of organization, it is economical.

7. **Direct Communication:** There is a direct relationship between the superior and the subordinate at all levels of organization. This will help to know each other intimately.

8. **Flexibility:** Adjustments in the organization can be easily made to suit the changing conditions of the business.

Demerits of Line Organization

1. **Lack of specialization**

Each person is responsible for the overall exhibition of

activities relating to his department alone. He is not expected to be an expert in all aspects of managerial task. He simply gives instructions to his subordinates and does not specialize in certain phases of operation.

2. Over loading

Whenever the scale of operations or size of the business unit increases, this system gives over work to the existing executives. So, they are not in a position to direct and control the efforts of their subordinates properly.

3. Lack of initiative

Since maximum authority is invested with the top management, the departments will lose their initiative to motivate the subordinates.

4. Scope for favoritism

Only one person controls the activities of the department when there is a scope for favoritism and nepotism.

5. Dictatorial

Under line organization, a subordinate should carry out the instructions and orders, which are given by the superior. If not, he will be penalized. This entails in autocratic and aristocratic approach in administration. So, managers will become dictators and not leaders.

6. Limited communication

In normal time, the communication moves downwards but very rarely it move upwards. The downward communication may be orders, instructions etc. If upward communication is allowed, the management may know the grievances of employees. But the top management does not prefer upward communication. So it results in limited communication.

7. Unitary administration

A single executive who takes all the decisions relating to his department looks after each department's activities. Hence, the successful functioning of that department depends on his abilities.

8. Subjective approach

The degree of availability of authority is more to the superior than to the subordinates. So the superior takes decision without considering the opinions of the subordinates. The subordinate should follow the decisions taken by the superior.

9. Instability

The success of this type of organization depends mostly on the ability of only a few strong men and the failure of this organization is likely due to the inability of the same persons.

10. Lack of co-ordination

The co-ordination among the departmental heads is not easy to achieve. The reason is that the executive of a department does not consider other departments important. This will result in the lack of co-operation and team spirit.

11. Unsuitability for large-scale enterprise

This type of line organization is not suitable for a large-scale enterprise, which requires specialization.

12. The business activities may be divided according to the will of the manager rather than according to any scientific plan.

13. The system has no means of appreciating the efficient worker and punishing of the inefficient worker.

14. Under line organization, efficient persons are essential to the top management. Practically, it is very difficult to find efficient persons for small organizations.

15. The required time and efforts are insufficient for managerial planning, research and development and controlling activities of the organization.

Suitability

1. This type of organization is suitable to small size business units.

2. Where the activities are of routine nature or machine based.

3. If the business activities are service minded.

4. Where the number of persons working is small.

5. The business operation is simple in nature.

6. A business unit, which has straight methods of operations.

12.2 Line and Staff Organization

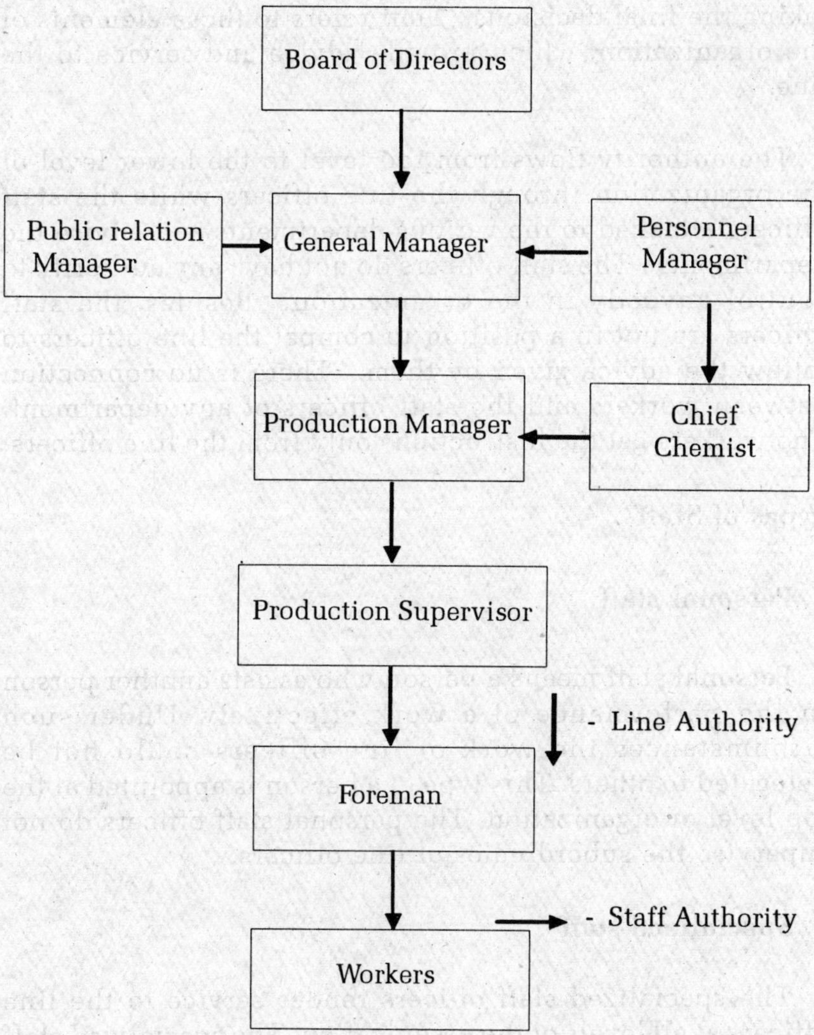

The line officers have authority to take decisions and implement them to achieve the objectives of the organization. The staff officers while framing the policies, plans and to take decision may assist the line officers. In the fast developing industrial world, the line officers are not in a position to acquire the technical knowledge. This type of gap may be bridged with the help of staff officers. The staff officers may be experts in a particular field. Then, the line officers can get expert advice from the staff officers before taking the final decisions. Staff refers to those elements of the organization, which provide advice and service to the line.

The authority flows from top level to the lower level of the organization through the line officers while the staff officers attached to the various departments and advise the departments. The staff officers do not have any authority to control anybody in the organization. Besides, the staff officers are not in a position to compel the line officers to follow the advice given by them. There is no connection between workers and the staff officers of any department. The workers get the instructions only from the line officers.

Types of Staff

1. Personal staff

Personal staff means a person who assists another person in the performance of a work effectively. Under such circumstances the work of line officers could not be delegated to others. This type of a person is appointed at the top level of organization. The personal staff officers do not supervise the subordinates of line officers.

2. Specialized staff

The specialized staff officers render service to the line officers at all levels of the organization. The specialized staff officers offer advice with some limited provisions. The management imposes these provisions.

3. General staff assistant

General staff assistants are a group of persons who are rendering service as advisors to top management in specialized matters. The primary feature of the general staff is that they give advice regarding overall plans and policies of the organization. But they are not specialized in any area.

Functions of Staff Officers

1. The staff officers assist the line officers in the planning of business activity.

2. The boards of directors frame the policies of the business on the basis of recommendations given by the staff officers.

3. The managers can get the advice from the staff officers regarding the selection, training, placement and remuneration fixation to the personnel.

4. The staff officers give advice regarding the method of improving the product, the technique of reducing the cost of production, increasing the profits of the concern etc.

5. The staff officers prescribe the procedures to be followed by the line officers in the execution of policies and programmes.

6. Staff officers of a department help the manager in the preparation of budget of the department.

7. The staff officers may be called to solve the administrative problems encountered by the line officers in general.

In many organizations, the line officers extend their full cooperation to staff officers and vice-versa. This ensures smooth functioning of the organization. In certain circumstances, conflicts may arise between the staff officers and line officers. When an officer blames the other officers for some lapse, it affects the smooth functioning of the business.

12.3 Arguments of Line Officers against Staff Officers

1. The staff officers have only theoretical academic knowledge but not practical knowledge.

2. Frequently, the staff officers go beyond their sphere of activity and assume that they have line officers' authority.

3. Much of the advice given by the staff officers is impractical.

4. Since the staff officers are not responsible for the results they suggest unfruitful ideas.

5. The staff officers unnecessarily increase the paperwork of the line officers.

6. The staff officers give advice without considering the nature of business as a whole.

7. The ideas of staff officers take into consideration only the objectives of the departments to which they are attached instead of the broad objectives of the business.

8. Staff officers are very much interested in becoming line officers of the organization rather than imparting advice to them.

9. Staff officers blame the line officers for the failure of the project but keen on getting credit for the success of the project.

12.4 Arguments of Staff Officers against Line Officers

1. The line officers completely neglect the advice given by the staff officers.

2. The line officers hesitate to accept new ideas.

3. The line officers do not follow the advice of staff officers properly.

4. Some line officers' simply reject the advice without considering its validity.

5. Some line officers are not ready to ask for any advice from the staff offices.

6. The line officers dissuade the management from giving authority to staff officers to implement new schemes.

7. The line officers do not exploit the full services of the staff officers.

12.5 Solution to the Conflict between Line Officers and Staff Officers

The conflict between line officers and staff officers can be settled: by the following suggestions.

1. Both line officers and staff officers should clearly understand the nature of relationship prevailing between them.

2. A separate staff member should be appointed to bring about cooperation between the line officers and staff officers.

3. The line officers should be encouraged to use the advice of staff officers.

4. Only qualified persons should be selected and placed as staff officers.

5. The staff officers should be convinced by the line officers if their advice is not accepted.

6. The responsibility for results could be fixed on both line officers and staff officers.

7. Some line officers may resist the change, then it is the duty of staff officers to encourage the line officers to participate in the proposed scheme of change.

8. Only experienced persons alone should be promoted as line executives.

9. The staff officers can give full credit to the line officers for the results Obtained.

10. Remove the fear of both line officers and staff officers whether the new ideas or advice would be properly put into use or not.

11. If the favorable results are obtained, the staff officers may be appreciated by the line officers.

12. A special privilege may be given to the line officers to reject or accept the advice given by the staff officers.

12.6 Advantages of Line and Staff Organization

1. It facilitates the workers to work faster and better.

2. Specialization is attained when the staff officers concentrate on planning the function and the line officers concentrate on execution function.

3. It enables the organization effectively to utilize the staff officer's experience and advice.

4. The line officers can take sound decisions with the help of proper advice from the staff officers.

5. A new technology or a new procedure may be introduced in the organization without any dislocation.

6. A new variety of responsible jobs can be given to skilled workers.

7. The work of line officers would be reduced to some extent if they are relieved of the work of taking decisions.

8. It promotes the efficient functioning of-the line officers.

9. The principle of unity of command is followed in the line and staff organization. Hence, the line officers can maintain discipline among the workers and exercise control over the workers.

10. A very good opportunity is made available to the young persons to get training.

12.7 Disadvantages of Line and Staff Organization

1. If the powers of authority pertaining to the line officers and staff officers are not clearly defined, there may arise confusion throughout the organization.

2. It is very difficult to control the line officers to when they reject the advice of the staff officers.

3. The line officers may reject the advice without assigning any reasons for their action.

4. The staff officers may under estimate the authority of line officers. The reason is that they are superior to the line officers.

5. The staff officers are-not involved in the actual implementation of the programme. So, it is not obligatory on their part to give advice with care and caution.

6. The staff officers are not responsible if favorable results are not obtained.

7. It requires the appointment of staff officers who are specialized in various areas. It increases the administrative expenses of the organization.

8. There is no authority to the staff officers to compel the line officers to accept and implement the advice given by them.

9. There is a communication gap between line officers and staff officers. It reduces the degree of co-operation between them.

10. The differences of opinion between line officers and staff officers will defeat the very purpose of specialization.

11. The line officers may misunderstand the advice given by the staff officers and proper results cannot be obtained. Sometimes, the staff-officers cannot give unambiguous advice to the line officers.

12. Line officers blame the staff officers for unfavorable results and want to get rewards for favorable results.

13. Frequently, the line officers want to get advice from the staff officers not only on important matters, but also on ordinary matters. It reduces the effectiveness of control of line officers.

Review Questions

Two mark question

1. What is Line organization?

2. What is the other name for Line organization?
3. What are the kinds of Line organization?
4. Highlight the Functions of staff officers?
5. What are the types of staff?

Part - B

1. Define Line and Staff concepts? Why has there been a conflict between line and staff in so many companies?
2. Line and staff conflict can be resolved through the exchange of line and staff positions so that managers understand each others roles, responsibilities and difficulties. Give your comments?
3. Highlight the Arguments of line officers against staff officers?
4. Highlight the Arguments of staff officers against line officers?

Chapter - 13

Decentralization

13.1 Decentralization

Definitions

Allen

Decentralization applies to the systematic delegation of authority in an organization context.

Koontz & O'Donnell

"Decentralization of authority is a fundamental phase of delegation"

Mc Farland

"It is a situation in which ultimate authority to command and ultimate responsibility for results is localized as far down in the organization as efficient management of the organization permits".

Meaning

Decentralization is the opposite of centralization. In a centralized set-up decision making authority is concentrated in a few hands at the top. It is the systematic and consistent reservation of authority at central points in the organization. In the decentralization, there is a dispersal of decision - making authority. It implies greatest powers to persons and places away from the centre.

13.2 Distinction between Delegation and Decentralization

S.No	Delegation	Decentralization
1.	It Acts as a process	It is the end results of delegation and dispersal of authority at various levels.
2.	It refers to the relationship between two individuals i.e. a superior and his immediate subordinate.	It refers to a relationship between the top management and various departments and divisions in the enterprise.
3.	Only through delegation of duties, subordinates can be involved in the activities aimed at the accomplishment of enterprise objectives.	The top management may or may not favour a deliberate policy to work for a general dispersal of authority.
4.	Control over a subordinate's performance is exercised by his superior who constitutes the source of delegation of authority.	Even the power to control may be delegated to the department concerned.

13.3 A Decentralized Enterprise

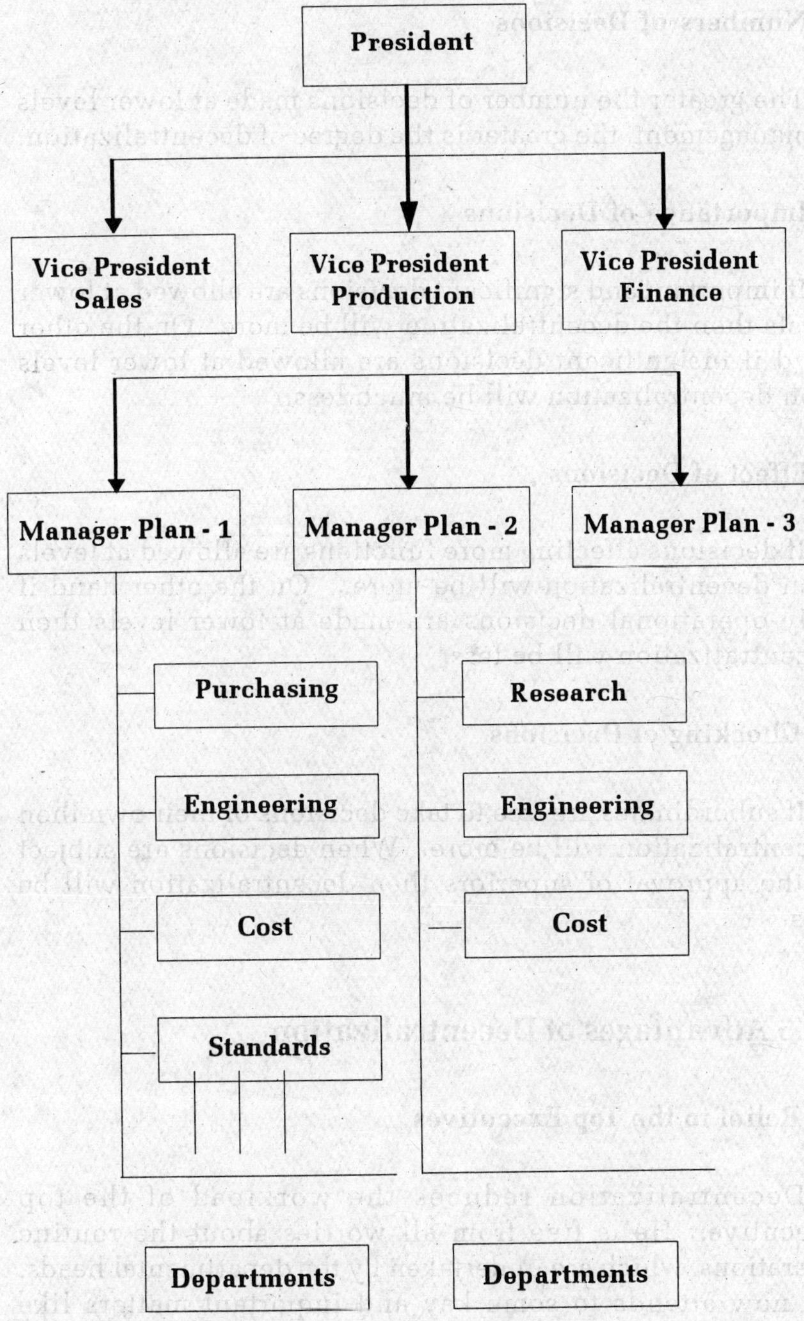

13.4 Measurement of Degree of Decentralization

1. Numbers of Decisions

The greater the number of decisions made at lower levels of management, the greater is the degree of decentralization.

2. Importance of Decisions

If important and significant decisions are allowed at lower levels then the decentralization will be more. On the other hand if insignificant decisions are allowed at lower levels then decentralization will be much less.

3. Effect of Decisions

If decisions affecting more functions are allowed at levels then decentralization will be more. On the other hand if only operational decisions are made at lower levels then decentralization will be less.

4. Checking of Decisions

If subordinates are free to take decisions of their own then decentralization will be more. When decisions are subject to the approval of superiors then decentralization will be less.

13.5 Advantages of Decentralization

1. Relief to the Top Executives

Decentralization reduces the workload of the top executive. He is free from all worries about the routine operations, which are undertaken by the departmental heads. He now attends to some key and important matters like planning, policy formulation, programme scheduling and decision making in key matters. He can fully utilize every minute at his disposal for the development of the organization. This makes him more alive, alert, smart and sharp.

2. Executive Development

When authority is decentralized, the subordinates get the opportunity of exercising their own judgment. They take initiative in developing their organization. They learn how to decide and how to manage. Thus, the problem of succession is overcome. Developing sound promotion and training policies fill up the managerial position from within. There is better utilization of lower level executives.

3. Growths and Diversification of Activities.

Decentralization facilitates growth and diversification of the activities. The authority facilitates addition of new product lines and taking the advantages of market conditions. Each product division is given sufficient authority for innovations and creativity. A sense of competition is created among different-divisions. It increases both productivity and profitability.

4. Quick Decisions

Decentralization facilitates quick decisions as authority to make decision is placed in the hands of those who are really responsible to execute to decision. As a result more accurate and faster decisions may be taken, as the lower level management is well aware of the realities of the situation. This avoids red tapism and delays.

5. Motivation of Subordinates

Decentralization promotes job satisfaction and improves

morale among lower level executives as they have greater opportunity of leadership and participation, which is reflected in better job performance. The local executives may foster team-spirit and group cohesiveness among the subordinates.

6. Effective Communication

Under decentralization, span of management is wider and there are fewer levels of organization. It develops intimate relationship between superior and subordinates including ineffective communication between the two.

7. Effective Supervision and Control

The greater the degree of decentralization, the more effective is the supervision and control. As the lower level executives have full authority in operation of activities, they can change work assignment or production schedules. They can recommend promotion of the subordinates and can take disciplinary action wherever necessary. It facilitates effective supervision. Control may also be made effective by evaluating the performance of each unit in the light of predetermined standards.

8. Management by objectives

Decentralization permits management by objective and self-control.

13.6 Disadvantages of Decentralization

1. Increase in administration cost

As each unit or division function self-sufficient, there are duplication of functions and under-utilization of facilities. This increases, administration cost.

2. Problem in coordination

If each division or unit enjoys autonomy it creates problem in co-ordination.

3. Lack of knowledge

It becomes difficult for the top management to know exactly what the lower level executives are doing or taking decisions.

4. Narrow Outlook

Executives at lower levels develop a narrow outlook, thinking only about the interest of their divisions or units to the detriment of the over-all interest of the organization.

5. Difficulties in emergencies

Emergency situations in a decentralized structure cannot be tackled properly. Adjustment to changing conditions may be difficult.

6. Inconsistencies

As uniform decision is not followed throughout the organization, each department may formulate its own policies and procedures.

7. Effect of external factors

Many external factors also make decentralization difficult such as market uncertainties, trade union movement government intervention etc.

13.7 How to Make Decentralization More Effective

1. Appropriate Centralization

There should be appropriate centralization to make decentralization more effective. Appropriate centralization means formulation of such policies and procedures, which concern the whole organization by which the control authority ensures uniformity of action and close co-ordination and control over the various operating units.

2. Centralized Control in Basic Areas

Centralized control in basic areas is necessary so that the top management may know where its various units are going. The control is mostly related to over all performance of a unit rather than interference in its day-to-day functioning. The unit manager must control these. Each unit must enjoy considerable autonomy within the framework of overall policy.

3. Development of Managers

The success of decentralization depends on the availability of quality managers in the organization who may successfully handle the unit independently. Better quality managers are always needed whatever the structure is adopted and they will show good results. Good managers can turn good result only when their abilities and potentials are properly utilized. Good quality managers cannot and should not be recruited from outside. They should be developed within the organization itself, by delegating authority and responsibilities and by allowing them to learn through experience in making decisions.

4. Competition among Units

As various units of a decentralized organization work

independently there should be proper competition among these units. The top management must develop such standards, which may evaluate the performance of each unit objectively and independently. Suitable incentive package may be adapted to reward highly efficient units. This will create team spirit among unit and department managers.

5. Open Communication

Open communication system should be established in the organization to ensure continuous interaction between the superior and subordinates. It must be a two-way communication. The superior should convey to subordinate executives necessary policies, framework and procedure to be adopted. Necessary advice and guidance should be given to subordinates from time to time. On the other hand, necessary feedback on operating results should be made available to superiors so that they may be aware of the real situation in the units to enable them to exercise control over them.

6. Effective Co-ordination

Decentralization tends to create rivalry and conflict among operating units. Department managers always complain of the scarce resources made available to them and try to grab a sizeable amount of the funds available by impressing the superiors. Therefore, effective co-ordination is necessary to prevent the danger of fragmentation, committees, liaison officers and other mechanism of coordination may be used to ensure effective co-ordination.

13.8 Making Organization Effective

In order to make organization effective, one should embark upon the common mistakes that occur in the process of organizing.

Common Mistakes in Organizing

1. Faulty Planning

A manager should plan for the right kind of organization structure that will serve the future, which will best serve an organization.

2. Lack of classification of relationships

The authority, responsibility, relationships must be clearly defined. Lack of clarification leads to a mere group of individual who are jealous, insecure and who are jockeying for position and favour.

3. Failure to delegate authority

This is a common complaint that is prevailing in most of the organizations. This leads to decision-making with many bottlenecks overburdening of top executives with many trivial issues and under nourishment of lower level managers.

4. Too much delegation

Excessive delegation leads to development of independent organizational satellites causing organizational failures. Some managers with excessive zeal to delegate their power do this. Too much delegation is also dangerous.

5. Adding people responsible who do not have authority

Superiors hold their subordinates responsible for results without giving them the authority to accomplish them. For this purpose, the superiors most clearly clarify the roles of their subordinates and give them sufficient authority.

6. Granting authority without exacting responsibility

A significant cause of mismanagement is the assignment

of authority without holding a person responsible. When authority is delegated to a subordinate, responsibility cannot be delegated. However, all the subordinates to whom authority has been delegated must be willing to be held responsible for their action.

Review questions

Two mark questions

1. Define Decentralization?

2. Distinguish between delegation and decentralization?

3. Draw a model of decentralizations enterprise of you own?

4. What are the advantages of decentralizations?

5. What are the limitations of decentralizations?

Part - B

1. How to make decentralization more effective?

2. Write short notes on (a) Advantages of decentralization (b) limitations of decentralization

3. Discuss the ways and means of Making Organization effective?

Chapter - 14

Organizational Culture

14.1 Organizational Culture

Definitions of Organizational Culture

Culture is something, which is created and resides in the minds of the people. Culture is, therefore, interpreted and defined differently by different people.

Edgar Schein who is the most closely associated with the study of organizational culture, defines it as "A pattern of basic assumptions invented, discovered, or developed by a given group as it learns to cope with its problems of external adoption and internal integration that has worked well enough to be considered valuable and, therefore, to be taught to new members as the correct way to perceive, think, and feel, in relation to those problems."

Turnstall defined organizational culture, as "A general constellation of beliefs, morals, value systems, behavioral norms, and ways of doing business that are unique to each corporation".

Recently, **Joanne Martin** while emphasizing differing perspectives of cultures in organizations, defined "As individuals come into contact with organizations, they come into contact with dress norms, stories people tell about what goes on, the organization's formal rules and procedures, its formal codes of behavior, rituals, tasks, pay systems, jargon, and jokes only understood by insiders, and so on. These elements are some of the manifestations of organizational culture".

One central theme flowing from above definitions is a system of shared meaning. This system of shared meaning is a set of key characteristics that the organization values.

Thus, organizational culture can be defined "as a pervasive underlying set of beliefs, assumptions, values, shared feelings and perceptions, which influence the actions and decisions taken by the organizations". The same distinguishes one organization from another.

Organizational culture is marked by a number of **characteristics.** Following are the most readily agreed upon ones.

1. Observed Behavioral Regularities

When people in the organization interact with one another, they generally use common language, terminology, and other rituals that relate to deference and demeanor.

2. Norms

Standards of behavior are set to guide the organizational members how much work to do. This, in many organizations, is expressed as "Do not do too much, do not do too little."

3. Dominant Values

Organizations advocate some major values and expect the same to be imbibed by its organizational participants. A few examples of such popular values are high product quality, regularity, and efficiency.

4. Philosophy

Organizations set forth certain beliefs about how employees and / or customers are to be treated.

5. Rules

There are guidelines prescribed how the new participants of the organizations have to adopt so as to be accepted the full-fledged members of their group in the organization.

6. Organizational Climate

This is an overall "feeling" that is conveyed by the physical layout, the way organizational participants interact with one another, and the mode organizational members conduct themselves with outside persons.

14.2 Types of Cultures

1. Dominant Culture and Subculture

The dominant culture gives a macro view of organization's personality. For example, most of the employees at the Reliance Group seem to share a concern for the value of the time. This creates a dominant culture in the organization that helps guide the day to-day behavior of employees.

A subculture expresses a set of values that are shared by the members of a division or department. Subcultures typically are a result of problems or experiences that are shared by members of a department or unit. These subcultures can form vertically or horizontally. When one product division of a conglomerate has a culture unique from that of other divisions of the organization, a vertical subculture exists. When a specific set of functional specialists such as accountants have a set of common shared understandings, a horizontal subculture is formed. It is important to mention that a particular department will include the core values of the dominant culture plus values distinct to the members of the particular department.

Strong and Weak Cultures: Based on intensity of shared ness, organizational cultures are of two types: strong and weak. A strong culture is characterized by the organization's core values being intensely held and widely shared. So to say, more intensely the core values are shared, the stronger the cultures. The degree of shared ness depends on two factors: orientation and rewards. In order for people to share the same cultural values, orientation programmes are organized to tell the new comers about the organization's philosophy and method of operation. Orientation may be done through both words-of-mouth and day-to-day work habits and examples. Rewards do also affect shared ness. For example, promoting employees those who hold the core values helps others as well better understand the core values. This, in turn, results in lower employee turnover. When core values are not, shared with high degree of intensity, it forms weak culture. Weak culture is usually characterized by high turnover of employees.

14.3 Functions of Culture

1. Culture provides shared patterns of cognitive perceptions or understanding about the values or beliefs held by the organization. This enables the organizational members how to think and behave as expected of them.

2. It also provides shared patterns of feelings to the organizational members to make them know what they are expected to value and feel.

3. It provides a boundary that creates distinctions between one organization and other. Such boundary defining helps identify members and non-members of the organization.

4. Culture facilitates the generation of commitment to something larger than one's individual self-interest.

5. It enhances social stability by holding the organizational members together by providing them appropriate standards for which the member should stand for.

6. It serves as a control mechanism that guides and shapes the attitudes and behavior of organizational members. It helps organizational members stick to the conformity to the prescribed and expected mode of behavior.

7. Culture finally, ensures that everyone is pointed in the same direction.

Culture exists in every organization. Now, the question that arises is whether it is good or bad. It is clear from the functions just outlined that culture is valuable for both the organization and the employee. Culture is valuable for the organization because it enhances organizational commitment of the employees. It guides employees how things are done and what is important for them.

14.4 Creating, Sustaining, and Changing a Culture

How is culture created? What forces sustain culture? And how does culture change? This section answers these questions one by one.

Creating a Culture

Beliefs and values have their base on the past happenings. It implies that the ultimate source of an organization's culture is its founders." The founders start their organization with a vision of what their organization should be. Then, the vision is imposed on all organizational members. The members imbibe the vision through interaction and their own experience. Thomas Watson of IBM is a good example.

Watson's views on research and development, product innovation, employees dress attire, and compensation policies still influence practices at IBM, though he died in 1956.

J.R.D. Tata is another example that typifies this type of culture creation. His supportive, consultive role, his belief on professionalism, and assumption that only honesty and fair dealings will pay have made the vast Tata Empire what it is today.

Luthans has outlined a distinct process involved-in the creation of a culture. The process involves the following steps:

1. A single person (founder) has an idea or vision for an enterprise.
2. The founder brings in some people and creates a core group that shares a common vision with the founder. All in the core group accept the idea or vision and work for it.
3. The founding core group begins to act in concert to create an organization by raising funds, obtaining patents, incorporating, locating space, building, and so on.

Sustaining a Culture

Culture once established may fade away also. Hence, once a culture is created, it needs to be sustained through reinforcement practices of human resources. Three such practices particularly important in sustaining a culture are selection practices, the actions of top management, and socialization methods. Let's take a closer look at each.

Selection: The first step involved in sustaining the culture is the careful selection of entry-level candidates. The basic purpose of selection process is to appoint right people for right jobs. For this, the trained recruiters interview candidates and attempt to screen out candidates whose personal styles and values do not make a fit with the organization's culture. Thus, by identifying the suitable candidates who can culturally match the organizational culture, selection helps sustain culture considerably.

Top Management: The actions of top management such as what the managers say and how they behave have a major impact on the employees working at lower levels. As a matter of fact, this filters down in the entire organization and becomes a common feature or culture of organization. Managerial actions like degree of freedom granted to the subordinates, prescriptions for the employee uniform, payoff in terms of pay raises, promotions, and other rewards also help create a common history i.e., culture in the organization.

Socialization: Socialization can be conceptualized as acquisition of work skill and abilities, adoption of appropriate role behaviors and adjustment to the norms and values of the work group. In simple words, socialization is the process of adaptation. New organizational members coming from different moods and mores are likely to disturb the common customs and beliefs already established in the organization Therefore; the new employees need to be indoctrinated to adapt the organizational culture. This adaptation process is called socialization. Socialization process involves three phases:

- Pre-arrival
- Encounter
- Metamorphosis

Pre-arrival refers to all the learning that occurs before a new member joins the organization.

Encounter is the stage of induction, which the new recruit, joins the firm and put on the job. The role-playing starts here. The recruit starts comparing expectations, the image, which he had formed during pre-arrival stage with reality. If expectation and reality concur, the encounter is smooth. But seldom it concurs. When the two differ, stress and frustration set in. What follows thereafter is a mental process of adjustment. In this adjustment, the individual try to replace his/her own values and norms with those of the organization at least in vital areas, if not in all. In the other extreme, the recruit simply cannot reconcile to those values and norms of the organization and get disillusioned and quit the job.

Metamorphosis is the completion stage of changes and consolidation of changed behavior (defreeze). In this stage, the employees master the skills required for their new roles, and make the adjustment to the organization's norms and values.

Changing a Culture

Culture established in one type of environment may not remain effective in changed environment. If it is so, the organization must either adapt to new conditions of environment or it may not survive. Hence, the need for change in organizational culture.

However, changing culture is as much important is not so easy or simple. Changing a strong culture is particularly difficult because the cultural values and assumptions have taken deep roots and employees become so committed to them. Yes, it is easier to change the culture when it is weak. Deal and Kennedy identified five situations, which facilitate change in the culture.

Delineates how culture is created and sustained through various forces

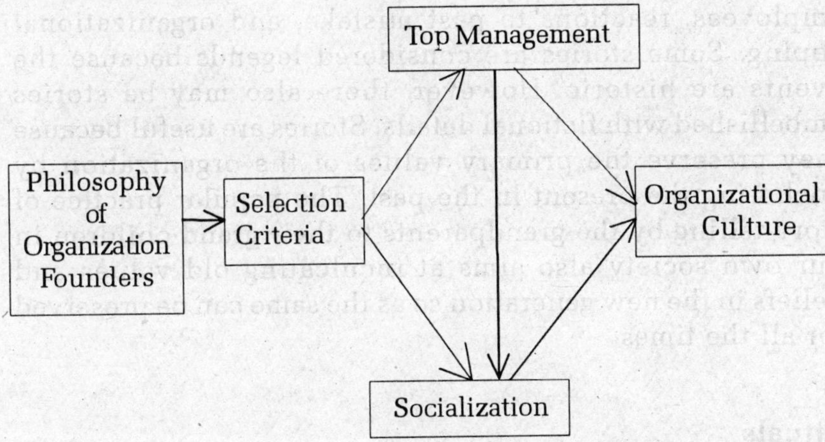

1. When the environment is going through rapid changes and the company has always been highly value-driven.
2. When the industry is highly competitive and the environment changes quickly.
3. When the company is mediocre, or worse.
4. When the company is truly at the threshold of becoming a large corporation.
5. When the company is growing very rapidly.

How is Culture Learnt?

The most potent ones are stories, rituals, symbols, and language.

Stories

Most stories are narratives based on true events about the organization's founders, rule breaking, rags-to-riches successes, reductions in the work force, relocation of employees, reactions to past mistake, and organizational coping. Some stories are considered legends because the events are historic. However, there also may be stories embellished with fictional details. Stories are useful because they preserve the primary values of the organization by anchoring the present in the past. The popular practice of story telling by the grandparents to their grand children in our own society also aims at inculcating old values and beliefs in the new generation so as the same can be preserved for all the times.

Rituals

Rituals also are a means for transmitting culture. Activities such as award ceremonies, weekly Friday picnic, and annual general meetings are some examples of rituals. These rituals reinforce the key values of the organization, what goals are important, which people are important and which are expendable.

Symbols

A symbol is something that represents something else. Physical symbols in organizations are often used to represent and support organizational culture. Examples of symbols include the size of offices, the elegance of office furnishings, executive perks, and the presence of reserved parking spaces for certain employees. The value of these symbols is that they communicate important cultural values. Symbols become more powerful facilitator of culture if symbols are consistent with the stories that are narrated to the organizational members.

Languages

As language is a means of universal communication, most organizations tend to develop their own language in the forms of jargon, phrases, acronym, slogans, etc. By learning this language, the members attest to their acceptance of the culture and, in so doing, help preserve the organizational culture.

Theorzy Z Culture

The remarkable economic success of Japanese firms influenced the U.S. organizations to imitate some selected Japanese practices, if not all. In consequence, some of the major American organizations such as IBM, Kodak, and Procter & Gamble attempted to adopt the Japanese management styles in their organizations. The American adaptation of the Japanese style of management is known as the "Theory Z Organizational Culture".

The overriding feature of a type Z organization is a feeling of cooperation and collaboration between managers and employees. In case of theory Z management structure, the employees feel a sense of equality and identity and also involvement as the partners of the organization. Employees have a better and greater understanding about one another's point of view, which serves a seedbed for shared norms and values in the organization. In summary, in the type Z organizations, employment is effectively a lifetime commitment. Consequently, employee turnover is low and employees' progress through a well-defined order of career positions over the period. Decision-making is done by consensus. There is a shared sense of collective responsibility for the success of a decision. The sense of collective responsibility increases productivity.

14.5 Comparison of Three Organizational Cultures

Type A (American)	Type J (Japanese)	Type Z (Modified American)
Short-term employment	Lifetime employment	Long-term employment
Individual decision	Consensual decision making	Consensual decision making
Individual responsibility	Collective responsibility	Individual responsibility
Rapid evaluation and promotion	Slow evaluation and promotion	Slow evaluation and promotion
Explicit, formalized control	Implicit, informal control with explicit, formalized measures	Implicit, informal control
Specialized career career path	Non-specialized specialized career path	Moderately path
Segmented concern	Holistic concern	Holistic concern, including family.

Review Questions

Two mark questions

1. Define Organizational Culture?
2. What is Dominant culture? Give example?
3. What is Subculture?

4. What are Strong and Weak cultures? Give example?

5. What is Socialization?

Part - B

1. Briefly explain how Culture is created and Sustained through various forces?

2. How Culture is learnt?

3. Bring out the Comparison of three Organizational culture?

Chapter - 15

Recruitment and Selection

15.1 Introduction

After the organization has determined the number and kinds of personnel needed by it, it should identify the sources from where they may be recruited. Recruitment would mean 'to obtain fresh supplies' or 'to restore' and 'replenish'. Recruitment means discovering applications for the present or future jobs in an organization. It also brings the job seeker and job giver closer together

Recruitment

15.2 Definitions

1. It is the discovering of potential applicants for actual (or) anticipated organizational vacancies.

2. It is a linking activity bringing together those with jobs and those seeking jobs.

3. It is a process to discover the sources of manpower to meet the requirements of the staffing schedule and to employ effective measures for attracting that manpower in adequate number to facilitate effective selection of an efficient working force.

4. It is the process of finding and attracting capable applicants for employment. The process begins when

new recruits are sought and ends when their applications are submitted.

Meaning

The purpose of recruitment is to locate sources of manpower to meet job requirements and job specifications.

Purpose and Importance of Recruitment

- Determine the present and future requirements of the organization in conjunction with its personnel. Planning and job analysis activities.
- Increase the pool of job candidates at minimum cost
- Help increase the success rates of the selection process by reducing the number of visibly, under qualified or overqualified job applicants.
- Help to reduce the probability that job applicants, once recruited and selected, will leave organization only after a short period of time
- Meat the organization legal and social obligations regarding the composition of its work-force
- Begin identifying and preparing potential job applicant who will be appropriate candidates.
- Increase organizational and individual effectiveness in the short term and long term.
- Evaluate the effectiveness of various recruiting techniques and sources for all types of job applicants.

15.3 Recruitment Process :

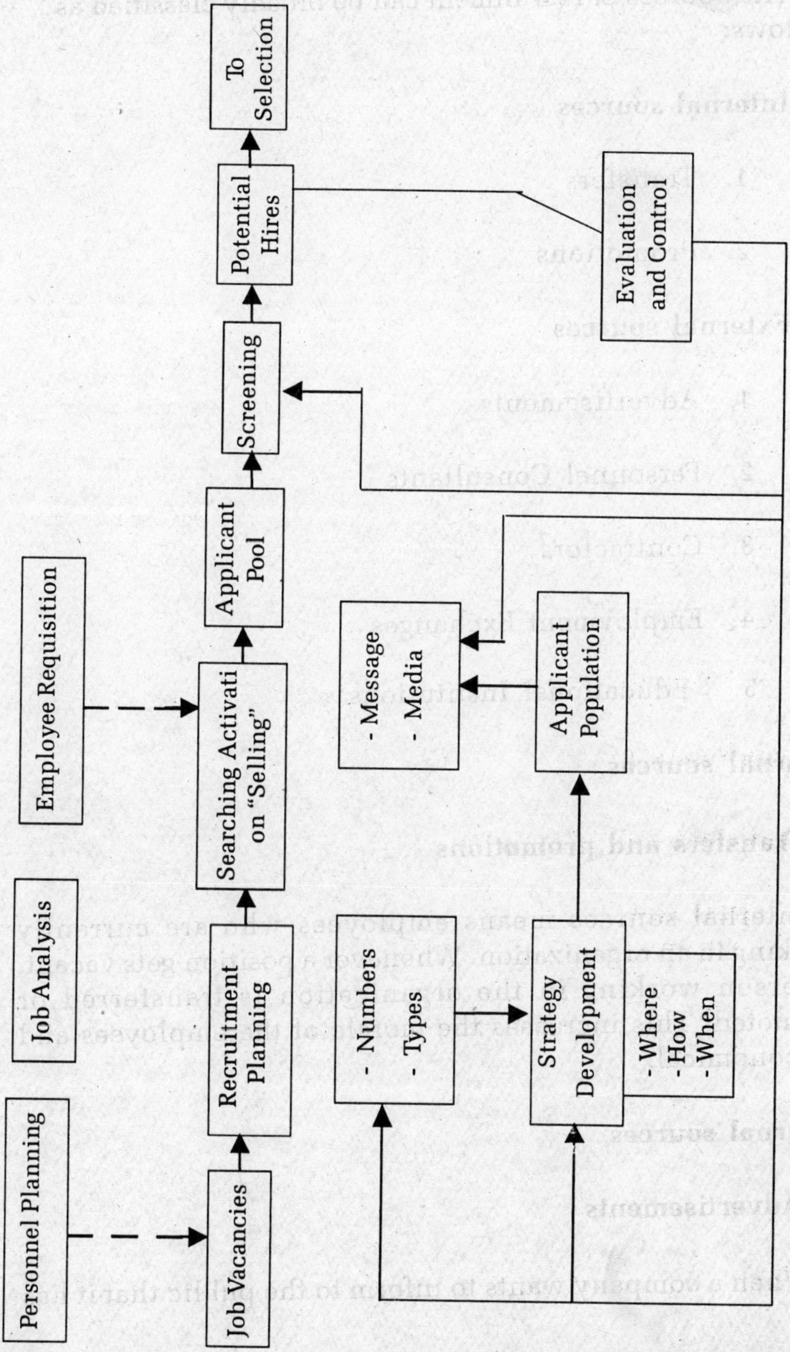

15.4 Sources of recruitment

The Sources of recruitment can be broadly classified as follows:

I. Internal sources

1. Transfers
2. Promotions

II. External sources

1. Advertisements
2. Personnel Consultants
3. Contractors
4. Employment Exchanges
5. Educational Institutions

Internal sources

1. Transfers and promotions

Internal sources means employees who are currently working in an organization. Whenever a position gets vacant, a person working in the organization is transferred or promoted. This increases the morale of the employees and is economical.

External sources

1. Advertisements

When a company wants to inform to the public that it has

a vacancy, it issues the advertisements. This contains a number of information on the job, location, remuneration and future job prospects. This method is costly, as the media rates have been increased. Many multinational organizations, advertise in journals like Business India, Business World, India today etc., in order to attract the attention of many managers working in other companies.

2. Personnel consultants

Consultants like ABC Consultancy acts as intermediary between the applicant and the enterprise. The consultant companies advertise in national Newspapers, screen, select the candidates and send them to the companies.

3. Employment exchange

Public employment exchanges serve as an important source of recruitment of people. They register the job seekers and pass them to employers. Generally unskilled and in experienced persons register their names with employment exchanges.

4. Educational institutions

Colleges, Universities offer opportunities to employers through their own placement departments, to recruit students freshly passing out of these Institutions. This facilitates the companies to conduct campus interviews and select the fresh candidates.

Recruitment Practices in India

Recruitment in Public Sector

1. Employment exchanges
2. Advertisements

3. Internal sources (Promotion & Transfer)

4. Casual employment seekers

5. Employees' relatives & friends

Recruitment in Private Sector

1. Advertisements

2. Employment exchanges

3. Relatives & friends of existing employees of their recommendations

4. Internal sources though promotion & transfers

5. Casual callers

Sons of the soil

- Persons from families who surrendered their lands for establishing the organization must be given first priority for employment with proper training.

- Selection committee be formed with a representative of State Government for filling up vacancies of lower level jobs

- Middle and higher level appointments be supervised by the public service commission

- Periodic return on status of employment be submitted to the Central and State Government

Methods of recruitment

- Direct method – Campus recruitment

- Indirect methods – advertisements in newspapers, Radio,T.V, journals, technical magazines etc
- Third party – Private employment agencies, management consultants, professional bodies / associations, employee referrals / voluntary organization / databanks.

15.5 Selection

Yoder

It is a process by which candidates for employment are divided into class – those who will be offered employment and those who will not.

Robbins

It is a process as to predict which job applicants will be successful if hired.

Koontz

It is a Process of choosing from among the candidates from within the organization or from the outside, the most suitable person for the current position or for the future position.

Stone

It is a Process of differentiating between applicants in order to identify and hire those with a greater likelihood of success in a job.

Meaning

It refers to the process of offering jobs to one or more applicants / candidates from the applications received through recruitment. It is the process of picking the suitable candidates from the pool of job applications to fill various jobs in the organization.

S.No	Recruitment	Selection
1.	It technically precedes Selection.	Selection follows recruitment
2.	Refers to the process of identifying and encouraging potential candidates to apply for jobs in the organization.	It involves choosing the best out of those recruited.
3.	Recruitment is positive as it aims at increasing the number of job seekers for wider choice or increasing the selection ratio.	It is said to be negative in its application as it rejects a large No of unqualified applicants to order to identify those who are suitable for the jobs.
4.	Recruitment involves searching	Selection involves comparing those already searched

15.6 Selection process

Selection means selecting the right candidates after receiving an adequate number of applications through different sources of recruitment. Selection involves a careful screening and testing of candidates who have sent their applications for a job in the Company.

1. Receipt and scrutiny of applications

Candidates with insufficient qualification and experience should be eliminated from the main list. This saves a lot of money and time for both the candidates and the company.

2. Preliminary interview

The objective of this is to see whether the applicant appears to be physically and mentally suitable for the job. The Questions relate to the Qualification, experience, age, residence etc.

3. Blank application forms

The blank application forms are collected from the candidates, to get the various details of candidates, which are related, to work experience, educational qualification, extra-curricular activities, references etc.,

4. Tests

The Tests are aimed at measuring such skills and abilities in a candidate. The tests are used to identify the intelligence, attitude, personality, interest etc. The tests also provide a good basis for measuring a candidate's suitability for the given jobs. The tests also help in establishing standards of job performance.

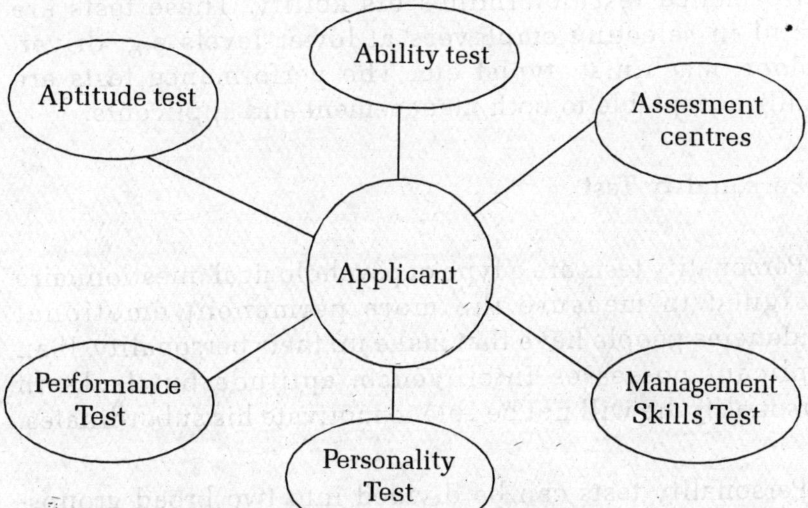

Tests used for selection

1. Ability Test

These are the tests that measure a candidate's existing ability, both mental and physical. They can measure a variety of areas, such as verbal reasoning, numerical ability. These are also called as performance tests. Such tests can be constructed entirely related to the job concern such as 'wiring, assembling, clerical, lecturing, musical, artistic etc.

2. Aptitude Test

Aptitude tests are designed to examine whether a candidate is likely to be able to acquire the skills and knowledge necessary to perform the job. Again, they can be set up as strictly job-related tests. An aptitude test is used to measure the job proficiency and job training of an employee.

3. Performance Test

When an applicant claims to know something, the performance test determines his ability. These tests are useful in selecting employees at lower levels e.g. driver, welder, machinist, typist etc. The performance tests are highly acceptable to both management and applicants.

4. Personality Test

Personality tests are a type of psychological questionnaire designed to measure the more permanent emotional tendencies people have that make up their personality. If an applicant possesses intelligence, aptitude but lacks in personality, he will not be able to motivate his subordinates.

Personality tests can be divided into two broad groups-first is normative tests designed to know the traits such as co-operative attitude, temper, emotional balance etc. The second is ideographic tests, which typically look at behaviors, ranking the strength of reaction to the different aspects. The ideographic test is also called as ispative test.

The ispative test is of objective type questions where candidates have to choose between a numbers of statements or adjectives that describe themselves.

The area of personality testing is one of the most sensitive areas in selection and is now under increased scrutiny. A candidate may say that he is a good organizer, forthright, focused, caring, relaxed and a great entertainer, but the test gives a much clearer picture of which are the strongest traits.

The personality tests are very useful in selecting marketing persons, salesmen, etc.

5 Interviews

An interview is a formal, face-to-face, observational and personal appraisal method to evaluate a candidate for a job. An interview is aimed at getting the maximum information about the candidate, giving the information about the company and motivating the candidate to join the company. Interview may be of various kinds like panel interview, stress interview, indirect interview etc.,

The interview is the most frequent method of selection. The interview is a fact-to-face conversation between an applicant and the employer. The purpose of interview is to collect information on behavior, attitudes, opinions, maturity, emotional stability, enthusiasm, confidence, response and other commercial behavior. The interview must be conducted professionally, usually involving more than one person to provide, a balanced assessment and counter criticisms of bias, involving line management and exploring techniques of questioning are all methods of improvement. The important factors considered at the time of interview are shown in the following figure

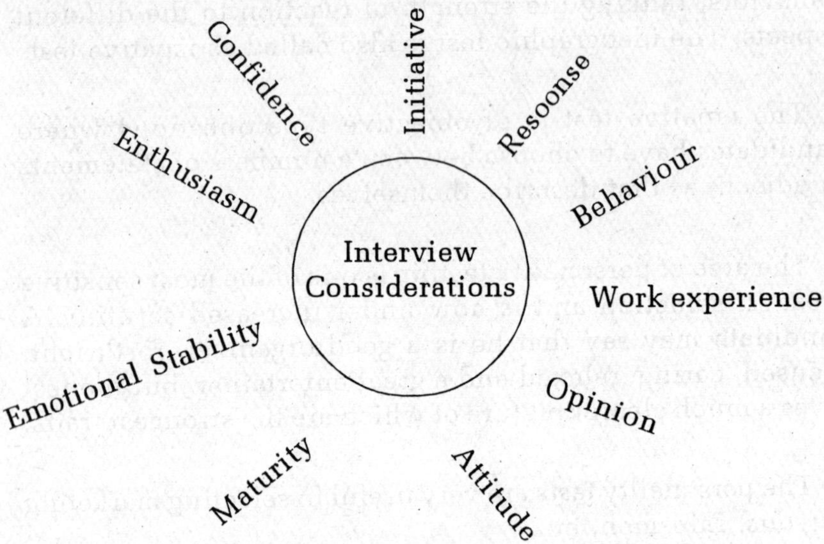

Advantages of Interview

1. Interview is a relatively low-cost exercise with additional expenses limited to the time of participants and traveling expenses.

2. No decision on selection should be taken without an interview.

3. Valid judgments like, inter-personal behavior, sociability, verbal fluency, confidence can be measured effectively in interview process.

4. A carefully and positively organized interview reflects good impression about the organization.

5. Interview gives the applicant a chance to learn the opportunities and job responsibilities that exists in the organization.

Types of Interview

For an effective and successful interviewing, a planned structure is necessary. Based on this the interviewing techniques can be categorized into three types

1. Structured Interview

Structured interview is also called as patterned interview. In structured interview, the interviewers are trained in the process to be used. In this type of interview, a list of questions based on analysis of the job specification is prepared. For these questions the applicant is evaluated on a standard point scale decided in advance. The interviewing process attempts to predict how candidates will perform in the work situation. A thorough and consistent approach is used for all the candidates. During the interview, no questions from the applicant are allowed.

2. Directed Interview

In directed interviewing face-to-face question answering takes place between employer and applicant. The questions related with job specifications, specific critical situation and work experience are asked. The directed interview assesses the candidate in respect of motivation, knowledge, capacity and personality.

3. Stress Interview

Some interviewers use stress questions as a part of an interview. The intention here is to examine how candidates react to an aggressive or to particularly critical remarks. Interviewers sometimes insult or try to humiliate the candidate. The candidate may answer in a matured way or may loose his temper and react accordingly. This is a controversial and risky strategy as the candidate, although dealing with the situation well, may not join the organization by being treated in this way.

4. References

Usually the names of three references are obtained from the candidates and letters are sent to these references asking for additional information. A verification of references might prove to be rewarding, as some candidates may provide incorrect information.

5. Selection and orientation

The candidates selected are subjected to medical examination and if qualified, the appointment orders are sent to them. The newly appointed people are given sufficient information of the rules, policies and procedures. They are also briefed with complete description of the jobs. The candidates are taken round the plant and introduced to various people. This gives sufficient knowledge of the company.

Review Questions

Two mark question

1. Define Recruitment?
2. Define Selection?
3. Distinguish between Recruitment and Selection?
4. Define the term Interview?
5. What are the advantages of Interview?
6. Highlight any two types of Interview?

Part - B

1. Briefly explain the Sources of Recruitment?
2. Define Selection? Outline a suitable selection process for a large business organization?
3. Point out the Sources of manpower recruitment? What sources will you prefer to managerial personnel and why?
4. Discuss the Major tests that are used in selection?

Chapter - 16

Performance appraisal

16.1 Performance appraisal

A performance appraisal is a process of evaluating an employee's performance of a job in terms of its requirements. It is the process employed for the purpose of placement, selection for promotions, providing financial rewards and other actions, which require differential treatment among the members of a group.

The term performance appraisal has been described as merit rating, behavioral assessment, employee evaluation, personnel review, progress report, staff assessment and service rating.

Performance appraisal has been considered as a most significant and indispensable tool for an organization. It is useful in making decision regarding various personnel aspects like promotions etc. They also help to pin point weak areas in the primary systems e.g. Marketing, Finance & Production. It is easier for managers to identify the group of employees who require training.

Douglas Mcgregor

Says, "Formal performance appraisal plans are desired to meet three needs, one of the organizations and the other two of the individual, namely:

1. To provide systematic judgments to back up salary increases, transfers, demotions or terminations.

2. They are means of telling a subordinate how he is doing and suggesting needed changes in his behavior,

attitudes, skiils, or job knowledge. They let him know "where he stands" with the boss.

3. They are used as a basis for coaching and counseling the individual by the superior.

According to Levinson, it seeks to provide an adequate feed back to each individual for his performance. It also serves as a lease for changing behavior.

The main objectives of performance appraisal are

1. To enable an organization to maintain an inventory of the number and quality of all managers and to identify and meet their training needs and aspirations.

2. To determine increments and provide a reliable index for promotions and transfers to positions of greater responsibility;

3. To maintain individual and group development by informing the employee of his performance standard.

4. To suggest ways of improving the employee's performance when he is not found to be up to the mark during the review period.

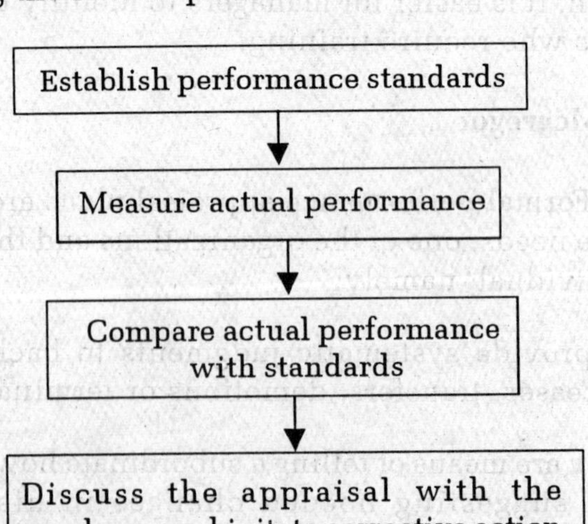

16.2 The process of evaluation

It begins with the establishment of performance standards to the employees and it should be communicated to the employees properly. It is necessary to acquire information in order to evaluate the performance of the employee. For measuring actual performance, personal observation statistical reports are used. The employees are now appraised and judged for future potential growth and advancement.

The deviation between the standard performance and actual performance is observed. Later the appraisal is discussed with employees for subsequent improvement and corrective action.

16.3 Career Strategy

Career strategy means helping the employees to plan their career in terms of their capacities with regard to the organizational needs. It includes establishing an organizational system of career movement and growth opportunities from the point of entry of an individual in employment to the point of his retirement. it is not only a series of work-related experiences, but also a series of properly sequenced role experiences, leading to an increasing level of responsibility, status, power, and rewards. it represents an organized path taken by an individual across time and space.

Today, in the changing scenario, the growing work expectations, and aspirations of employees, the career strategy is an essential prerequisite for effective man-management, organizational growth and optimum productivity.

Advantages of Career Strategy

1. It increases the utilization of managerial reserves within the organization.

2. It ensures satisfactory performance of employees by meeting their needs and aspirations for growth.

3. It reduces the employee turnover for lack of promotional avenues.

4. It improves and maintains motivation and morale of employees.

5. The career strategy helps a person to know in advance the level to which he can rise if he has the ability and aptitude for it.

6. It makes an organization to have a better image in the employment market, and it will attract and retain competent people.

7. It contributes towards individual development and utilization as well as to organizational development and effective achievement of corporate goal.

Limitations of Career Strategy

1. Small organization cannot have career strategy only large organization can opt for it.

2. It will not serve the purpose when the employees are illiterates, less educated, and perform jobs for which labour supply is abundant.

3. The absence of integrated personnel policy and plans which is quite common in Indian enterprises.

4. The members of a family expect to move faster than their professional colleagues in the career ladder. Thus the growth expectations of the members of the family may upset the career exercise.

5. It may not be effective if it is attempted for a period exceeding a decade.

16.4 Job Enrichment

Job enrichment tries to embellish the job with factors that Herzberg characterized as motivators such as a achievement, recognition, increased responsibilities, opportunities for growth, advancement and increased competence. It is therefore, based on the assumption that in order to motivate personnel, the job it self must provide opportunities for achievement and growth. Job enrichment has four unique aspects

1. It changes the basic relationship between employees and their work.
2. It changes employee behavior in ways that gradually leads to more positive attitudes about the organization and better self image.
3. It helps the employer to bring about the organization changes easily, securing employee co-operation and commitment
4. Job enrichment can humanize an organization individual are encouraged to grow and push themselves.

16.5 Organizational Development (OD)

Definitions

It can be defined as the application of planning, development and problem solving process to the overall functioning of the organization in such a way that it strengthens the physical, financial, human resources factors and improves the process of interpersonal relationship of the organization.

According to Bennis " Organizational Development is response to change, a complex educational strategy intended to change the beliefs, attitudes and structure of organization so that, they can better adapt to new technologies, markets and challenges.

Wendell Franch observes that "O.D. refers to a long range effort to improve an organisation's problem solving capabilities and its ability to cope with changes in its external environment with the help of external or internal behavioural scientists, consultants, or change agents".

According to Blake and Mounton "O.D.is a systematic way of introducing change based on a structural model for progressing in a programmatic sequence of steps from individual learning to organization application focused upon those silent and often negative attributes of culture which dictate action that so frequently contradict business logic with emphasis on confronting and resolving conflict as a prerequisite to valid problem solving and employing a variety of techniques of organizational study and learning to bring about the necessary change".

Objectives of Organizational Development

1. To increase the level of trust and support among organizational members.
2. To increase the incidence of confronting organizational problem both within groups and among groups, in contrast to "Sweeping Problems under the rug"
3. To increase the openness of communications laterally, vertically and diagonally.
4. To increase the level of personal enthusiasm and satisfaction in the organization.
5. To find synergistic solution to problem with greater frequency.

6. To increase the level of self and group responsibility in planning and implementation.

7. To improve organization's capability to cope with changing environment.

8. To move toward high collaboration and low competition between interpendent units.

9. To create conditions where conflict is effectively managed.

10. To enhance identification of the members and groups with the organizations.

16.6 Characteristics of O.D

i. Decision making on the basis of competence rather than authority.

ii. Creatively resolving conflict and designed to replace win – lose situations with win – win types.

iii. Reducing dysfunctional commitment and a sense of ownership of organization throughout the workforce.

iv. Increasing commitment and a sense of ownership of organization throughout the workforce.

v. Increasing the degree of interpersonal trust and support.

vi. Creating a climate in which human growth development and renewal are a natural part of the enterprise's daily operation.

Factors	Management Development	Organizational Development
Objectives	Improving managers contribution to goal accomplishment	Change the nature of the organization.
Focus	Train and Equip employees and manager focus an achieving existing organization.	Focus on design, not on the managers to perform better in improvements in design.
Approach	Educative and training	Problem solving approach
Time	Short-Range	Long-range strategy for organization innovation and renewal
Specialist	No special requirements	Trained specialist required

Review Questions

Two mark questions

1. Define Performance Appraisal?
2. What is the Main Objective of Performance appraisal?
3. Define Career?
4. Define Organizational Development?
5. Distinguish between Management Development and Organizational Development?

Part - B

1. What is Performance Appraisal and Discuss the Process of performance appraisal?

2. What are the Advantages and Disadvantages of career strategy?

3. What are the main features of Organizational Development?

4. "Organization Development involves development of the organization in the light of its future plan" Discuss?

Chapter - 17

Directing

Motivation and Leading

17.1 Introduction

Managing requires the creation and maintenance of an environment in which individuals work together in groups towards the accomplishment of a common objective. A manager cannot do this job without knowing what motivates people? Why do people do certain activities at a particular point of time? The answer to these questions is motives. Motive is the inner state that energies a person, that activates and channels behaviors towards goal.

Leaders are a key human resource in any organization. We usually think of companies competing by means of their products, but they probably compete more by means of their leaders than by their products. Better leaders develop better employees and two together develop better products. Therefore an employer who develops better leaders contributes more to the society and gains a competitive advantage.

In order to accomplish the organizational goals, the managers have to frequently communicate their employees the necessary information, decisions, ideas, suggestions and so on. The success of an organization depends a great deal on effective communication.

17.2 Definitions

Fred Luthans

"Motivation is a process that starts with a Physiological or Psychological deficiency or need that activates behaviors or drive that is aimed at a goal or incentive"

Stephen. P. Robbins

"Motivation is the willingness to exert high levels of effort toward organizational goals, conditional by the effort and ability to satisfy some individual need".

Gray

"The result of processes, internal or external to the individual, that arouse enthusiasm and persistence to pursue a certain course of action".

Beach

"Motivation means a willingness to expand energy to achieve a goal or a reward.

Shartle

"Motivation means a reported urge or tension to move in a given direction or to achieve a certain goal".

Scott

"Motivation means a process of stimulating people to action to accomplish desired goals".

S.Zedeck

"Motivation is a Pre-disposition to act in a specified goal directed way".

Meaning

Motivation originally comes from the Latin word mover, which means to move. It is derived from the word motive. Motivation refers to goal – directed behavior. It applies to the entire class of drives, desires, needs, wishes and similar forces that induce an individual or a group of people to work.

17.3 The process of Motivation

An unsatisfied need creates tension that stimulates drives within the individual. These drives generate a search behavior to find particular goals that if attained, will satisfy the need and lead to the reduction of tension.

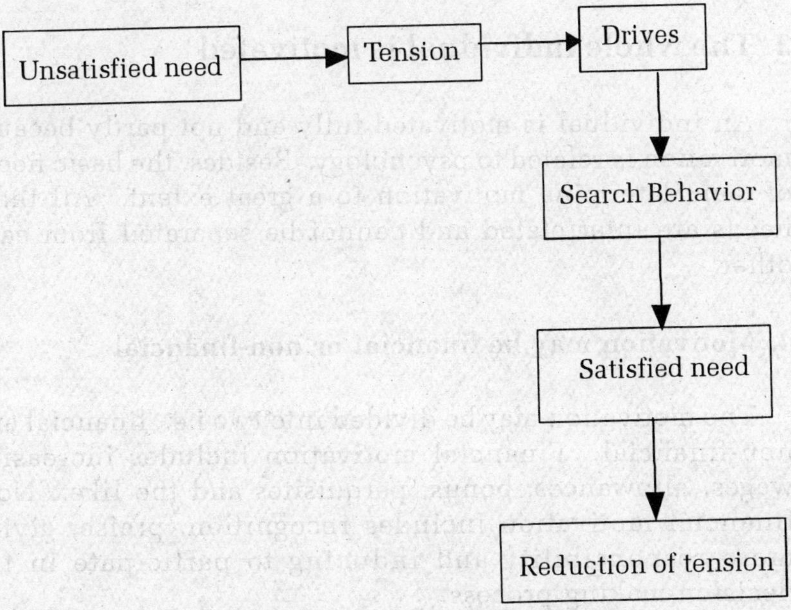

17.4 Nature of Motivation

Motivation is concerned with the direction of functions of management, so the nature of motivation can be understood from the following points.

1. Unending process

A social animal (a man) has number of wants. These wants induce a man to work. All the wants cannot be satisfied at one time. If one want is satisfied, then another want emerges. Motivation is also an unending process just like the satisfaction of wants is an unending process.

2. A psychological concept

Motivational deals with the psychology of workers. An efficient worker will not perform the work desirably well unless he is properly motivated. So, effective performance requires proper motivation. Proper motivation is possible only though proper analysis of the psychology of workers.

3. The whole individual is motivated

An individual is motivated fully and not partly because motivation is related to psychology. Besides, the basic needs of man determine motivation to a great extent. All these needs are interrelated and cannot be separated from each other.

4. Motivation may be financial or non-financial

The motivation may be divided into two i.e., financial and non-financial. Financial motivation includes increasing wages, allowances, bonus, perquisites and the like. Non-financial motivation includes recognition, praise, giving more responsibility and inducing to participate in the decision-making process.

5. Frustrated man cannot be motivated

If a man does not have his basic needs satisfied, he may be frustrated. He may be mentally ill to some extent. Such a frustrated man cannot be motivated unless his basic needs are satisfied.

6. Goal are motivators

Man works to achieve his individual goals. Whenever the goal is achieved, he will be no longer interested to work. So, the management should identify the goals of individuals, and it can persuade them to work by directions.

7. Unifying force

Unifying force means the drive to actualize one's own image. The person's self image plays an important role in motivation. If an individual has created an image as a leader, he acts accordingly. So, the unifying force is an important motivating force.

8. Motivation can be positive or negative

Positive motivation means use of incentives. The incentives may be financial and non-financial. Pay revision, confirmation of job and the like are positive motivations. Negative motivation means emphasizing penalties. Demotion and termination from the service are some of the examples of negative motivation.

9. Motivation and job satisfaction are different

Motivation is goal-oriented behavior. Job satisfaction is the outcome of a job performance. So, motivation is entirely different from job satisfaction.

Importance of Motivation

A manager guides the people in a desired manner in order to achieve organizational objectives. Two important things are necessary to perform any job. People have ability to work and willingness to work. Unwillingness to work is of no use. Hence, there is a need for motivation to create willingness in the minds of workers to do a job. So, the performance may be expressed in the following formula

Performance = ability X motivation (willingness)

E.F.L. Brech has explained the importance of motivation as "The problem of motivation is the key to management actions and in its executive form; it is among chief tasks of the general manager. We may safely lay it down that the tone of an organization is the reflection of the motivation from the top".

The importance of motivation is briefly discussed below

1. Maximum utilization of factors of production

Workers perform the work sincerely through the inspiration of motivation. This creates the possibility of maximum utilization of factors of production viz., labor and capital.

2. Willingness to work

Motivation influences the willingness of people to work. A man is technically, mentally and physically fit to perform the work but he may not be willing to work. Motivation creates a willingness on the part of workers to do the work in a better way.

3. Reduced absenteeism

Financial incentive schemes coerce the workers to work

more. Financial incentive scheme is framed in such a way that monetary benefits are given on the basis of number of hours engaged. This reduces absenteeism

4. Reduced labor turnover

Motivation has both financial and non-financial incentive schemes. This helps to retain the existing labors. The enterprise can plan its activities on long-term basis with the help of reduced labor turnover.

5. Availability of right personnel

Financial and non-financial incentives not only retain the existing employees but also attract the employees from outside the enterprise. In other words, right people are attracted from outside to work for the enterprise.

6. Building of good labor relations

Motivation helps to solve the labor problems of absenteeism, labor turnover, indiscipline and grievances. This ensures building of good labor relations.

7. Increase in the efficiency and output

Both workers and management have got benefits from motivational plans. On the one hand, wages of the workers increase corresponding to the increase of output and efficiency. On the other hand, the productivity of the organization and its profits increases due to consolidated efforts of the motivated people.

8. Sense of belonging

A proper motivation scheme promotes closer rapport between enterprise and workers. The workers begin to feel that the enterprise belongs to them and consider its interests as their own. Thus, there is no difference between workers and enterprise.

9. Basic of co-operation

Efficiency and output are increased through co-operation. The co-operation could not be obtained without motivation, so, motivation is a basis of co-operation.

10. Helps in realizing organizational goals

Organizational goals are achieved quickly through motivation. Motivated employees have a feeling of total involvement in the performance of organization task. Employees may work wholeheartedly for the realization of organizational goals.

11. Improvement upon skill and knowledge

Employees have promised efficient job performance. Hence, the employees may improve upon their skill and knowledge required for the job.

17.5 Types of Motivation

1. Negative motivation

Negative motivation is based on force of fear. If the worker fails to complete the work, they may be threatened with demotion, dismissal, lay-off, pay-cut, etc. The negative motivation gives maximum benefits in the short-run. In the long run, there are no such benefits available to the organization. Negative motivation results in disloyalty to the group as well as to organization.

2. Positive motivation

Positive motivation is based on rewards. According to Flipps, "Positive motivation is a process of attempting to influence others to do your will through the possibility of gain or reward. "Praise, participation in decision-making process, pride and delegation of authority and responsibility are some of the methods of positive motivation.

3. Extrinsic motivation

Motivation is available only after the completion of a job. Increase in wages, retirement benefits,rest periods, holidays, health wages, health insurance and the like are examples of extrinsic motivation.

4. Intrinsic motivation

Intrinsic motivation is available at the time of performance of work. These motivations provide a satisfaction during the performance of the work itself. Praise, recognition, power, delegation of authority and responsibility, competition and participation in the decision-making process are some of the examples of intrinsic motivation.

5. Financial motivation

Financial motivation is directly or indirectly associated with money. The most important financial motivations are wages and salaries. Bonus, profit sharing, vacation pay, free-medical services, retirement benefits and insurance are some of the other financial motivations.

6. Non-financial motivation

Non-financial motivation is that motivation which is not associated with monetary rewards. Praise, job rotation, delegation of authority and responsibility, participation, recognition and power are some of the examples of non-financial motivation. According to Robert Dulin, "Non-financial incentives are the psychic rewards or the rewards of enhanced position that can be secured in the work organization".

17.6 Theories of Motivation

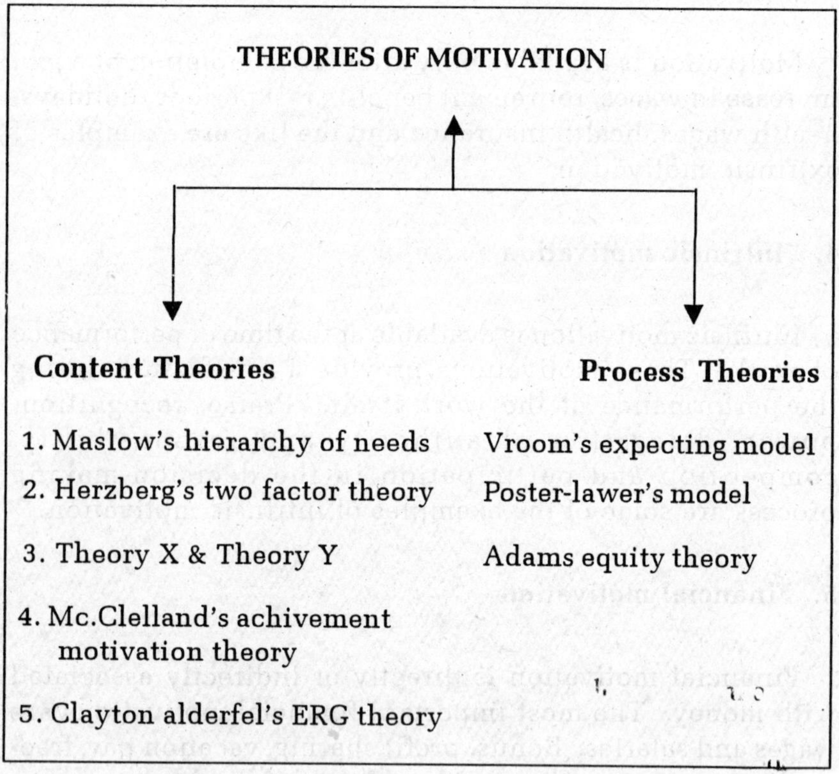

Theories of Motivation

Maslow's need hierarchy theory (1943) Maslow examine the question why people work in terms of their need satisfaction or need deprivation. His theory postulates that human needs can be organized into a hierarchy of prepotency with the physiological needs at the bottom and self-actualization at the top. He presents five needs categories.

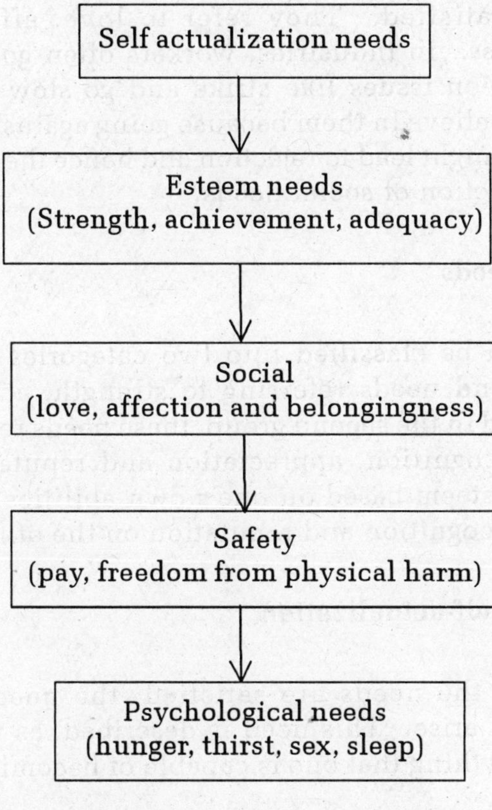

a. Physiological needs

These refer to the basic needs for the maintenance of body processes, such as hunger, thirst, sex and sleep. When these needs are satisfied, the higher order needs emerge, which dominate a person's behavior.

b. Safety needs

These refer to needs like freedom from physical harm, need for orderly life, and economic security.

c. Social needs

Social needs emerge when the psychological and safety needs are satisfied. They refer to love, affection and belongingness. In industries, workers often go along with their groups on issues like strike and go slow even when they do not believe in them because going against the wishes of the group might lead to rejection and hence the deprivation of the satisfaction of social needs.

d. Esteem needs

These can be classified into two categories-in the first group, we find needs referring to strength, achievement, adequacy and in the second group, these needs relate to such things as recognition, appreciation and reputation. Man values self-esteem based on one's own abilities on the one hand, and recognition and reputation on the other.

e. Need for self-actualization

When all the needs are satisfied, the need for self - actualization arise. This need is described, as the need to become everything that one is capable of becoming.

As each need becomes satisfied, the person steps up into the next higher need. i.e., the person moves up the hierarchy. As wants and needs are unlimited, one can say that no need is ever fully gratified. Maslow estimated that, the lower level needs which are satisfied externally, generally are satisfied to the tune of 85% of basic needs and 70% of security needs. But the higher order needs, which are satisfied internally, are satisfied to the tune of 50% of the belongingness need, 40% of esteem needs, and a mere 10% of the self-actualization needs.

In a nutshell, Maslow saw Human needs in the form of a hierarchy, ascending from the lowest to the highest, and he concluded that when one set of needs was satisfied, this kind of need ceased to be a motivator.

Critical appraisal of Maslow's theory

There is little empirical evidence in support of this theory. Maslow himself asserts that the theory is primarily, a framework for future research.

The criticism raised against Maslow's theory is that this mode lf motivation doesn't handle the problem of linkage between individual need satisfaction and the achievement of organizational objectives.

For e.g.: the objective of an organization is "Increased-productivity". At the same time the workers are asked to produce high quality products in order to cut down the final rejection rate. In this case the workers might be deriving more need satisfaction from making higher quality product at the cost of quality.

Yet another criticism leveled against Maslow's theory is non-accountability of individual differences in motivation. Maslow's himself explained that his model may not hold good for persons with particular experiences. His theory thus becomes non-predictive because data that do not support it can be interpreted in terms of individual differences.

Despite these criticisms this theory has some implications for management practices. It implies that in order to get the maximum from the worker, the organization has to attempt to satisfy higher order needs and that the organization concern for the satisfaction of lower order needs need not be overly stretched because a fully satisfied need doesn't fully motivate.

Herzberg's two factor theory of motivation or Hygiene theory

This theory of motivation-hygiene was proposed by psychologist Frederick Herzberg who asked a basic question to 200 accountants and engineers in firms in and around Pittsburgh-"What do people want from their jobs"? He used the 'Critical Incident method' of obtaining data for analysis. The critical incident was described as Think of a time when you felt exceptionally good or exceptionally bad about your job, either your present job or any other job you have had".

The responses obtained were interesting and fairly consistent. Generally good feelings were associated with job content. The bad feelings on the contrary were associated with job context. Herzberg concluded that job satisfaction is related to job content and job dissatisfaction were also related to job content.

As seen in figure certain characteristics tend to be consistently related to job satisfaction (factors on the right side of the figures), and others to job dissatisfaction (the left side of the figure). Intrinsic factors, such as achievement, recognition, the work itself, responsibility, advancement, and growth seem to be related to job satisfaction. When those questioned felt good about their work, they tend to attribute these characteristics to themselves. On the other hand, when they were dissatisfied, they tend to cite extrinsic factors, such as company policy and administration, supervision, interpersonal relations and working condition.

According to Herzberg, the factors leading to job satisfaction are separate and distinct from those that lead to job dissatisfaction. Therefore, managers must try to eliminate factors that create job dissatisfaction and bring peace. But he cannot motivate them. As a result, such factors such as company policy and administration, supervision, interpersonal relations, working conditions and salary have been called Hygiene factors. When they are adequate, people will not be dissatisfied, and however neither will they be satisfied.

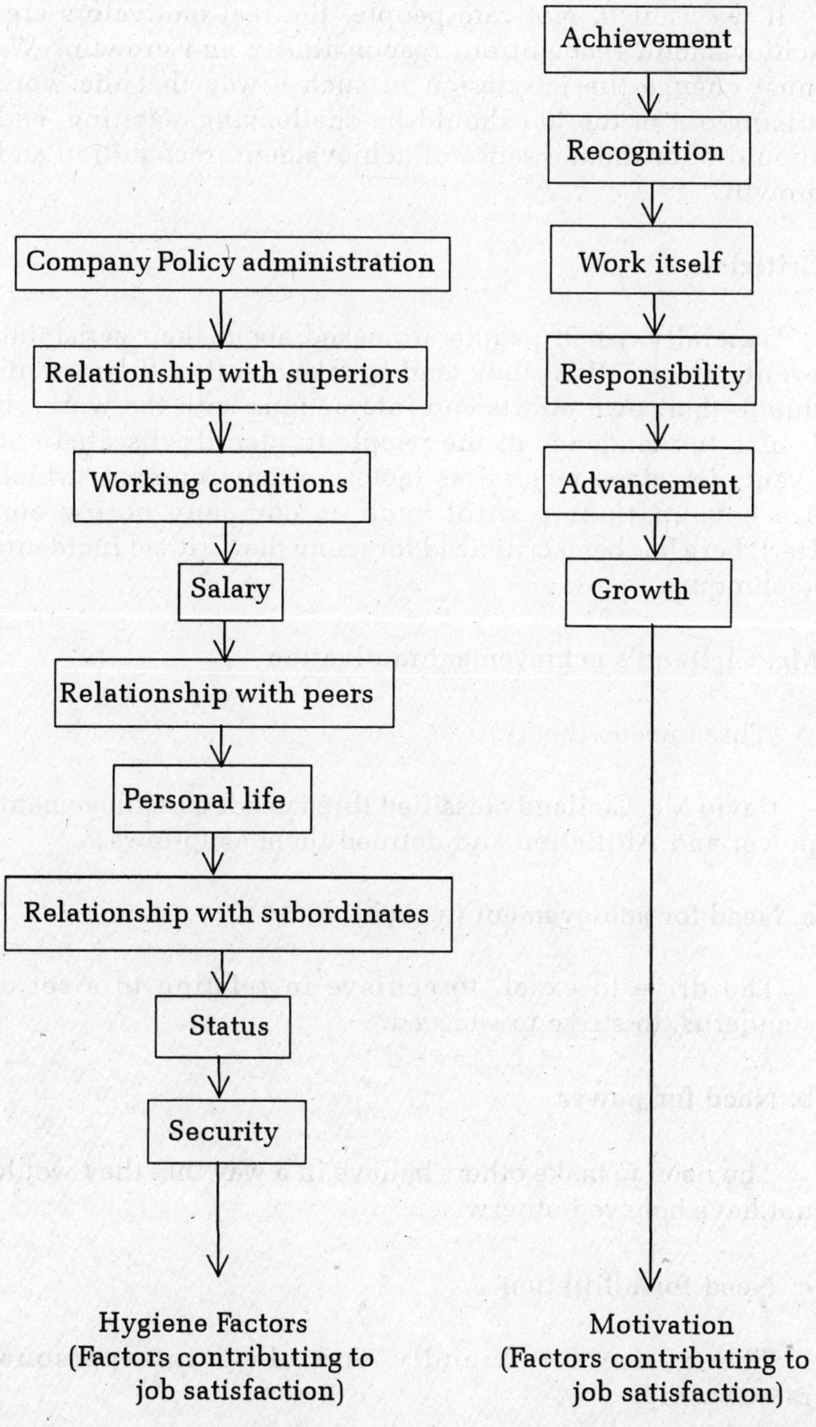

Achievement
Recognition
Work itself
Responsibility
Advancement
Growth
Company Policy administration
Relationship with superiors
Working conditions
Salary
Relationship with peers
Personal life
Relationship with subordinates
Status
Security
Hygiene Factors
(Factors contributing to
job satisfaction)
Motivation
(Factors contributing to
job satisfaction)

If we want to motivate people, the real motivators are. achievement, recognition, responsibility and growth. We must change the job design in such a way that the work arising out of the job should be challenging, exciting, and should offer them a sense of achievement, recognition and growth.

Criticism

Generally, when people are asked about their satisfying events, (motivation) they tend to take credit of their events due to their own efforts and interactions with the work. It is also the tendency of the people to identify dissatisfying events (Hygiene factors) as factors of environment, which are beyond their control such as company policy etc. Hertzberg has been criticized for using the 'Critical Incidents Techniques'.

Mc. Clelland's achievement motivation

(Three needs theory)

David Mc. Clelland classified three needs as achievement, power and Affiliation and defined them as follows.

a. Need for achievement (n. Ach)

The drive to excel, to achieve in relation to a set of standards, to strive to succeed.

b. Need for power

The need to make others behave in a way that they would not have behaved otherwise.

c. Need for affiliation

The desire for friendly and close interpersonal relationships.

According to Mc. Clelland, people can be classified into two groups, one small and the other large: Those falling in the small groups are challenged by opportunities and the other is not so challenged by opportunities. Mc. Clelland arrived at this conclusion by asking a number of people to write stories about and around a number of relatively unclear pictures. Everyone gave his own story, projecting the inner feelings, hopes, likes, aspirations, likes and dislikes. These stories were evaluated on the basis of success, competitiveness and excellence.

The high achievers projected the following traits

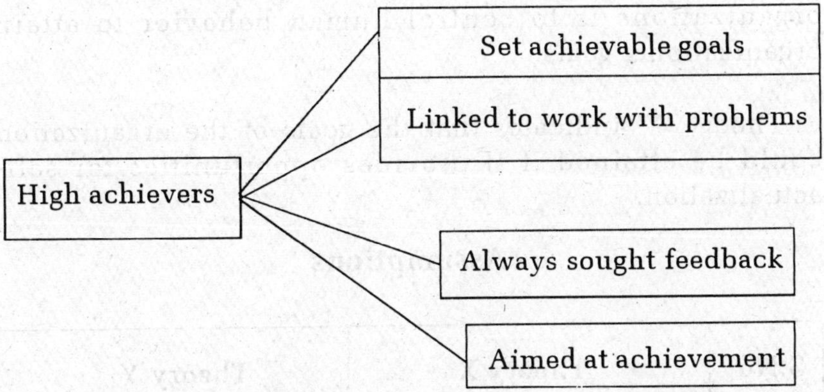

Findings

High achievers are successful as entrepreneurs because managing their own business, give the satisfaction of personal achievement.

People with high achievement need may or may not be good managers because in large companies, managing is a question of making others achieve their targets rather than personal goal achievement.

People with high power need are successful as managers, because the desire for power drives others to work.

Employees can be successfully trained for high achievement where the jobs actually require high achievers. But people with high aptitude for achievement need alone can be trained.

Mc. Gregor's Theory 'X' and Theory 'Y'

Mc. Gregor (1960) makes two sets of assumptions underlying theory 'X' and theory 'Y'. The two sets are opposites. These assumptions reflect the basic contradiction in human nature.

Theory 'X' states that the role of managers and organizations is to control human behavior to attain organizational goals.

Theory 'Y' indicates that the goals of the organization could be attained if it provides opportunities for self-actualization.

Assumptions

S.No	Theory X	Theory Y
1.	Work is inherently distasteful to most people.	Work is natural as play if the conditions are favorable.
2.	Most people are not ambitious, have little desire for responsibility and prefer to be directed.	Self-control is often indispensable in achieving organizational goods
3.	Most people have little creativity in solving organizational problems	The Capacity for creativity in solving organizational problems is widely distributed among people.

4.	Motivation occurs only at the physiological and safety levels	Motivation occurs at the social esteem and self-actualization levels as well as physiological and security levels.
5.	Most people have to be closely controlled and often coerced to achieve organizational goals.	People can be self-directed and creative at work if properly motivated.

Briefly, theory X assumes that most-people, in general, dislike work and need to be coerced and controlled to make sure that they put sufficient efforts to achieve the organizational goals. Mc. Gregor feels that it is not inherent in Man to dislike work. It is a product of the nature of the organization, management philosophy, policies and practices.

So, for managing people Mc. Gregor suggested his theory 'Y'. The broad dimensions of the theory are as follows;

Management is responsible for organizing the elements of productive enterprise in the interest of economic ends. People are not by nature passive. They become so as a result of experience in organization.The motivation is the potential for development. It is the responsibility of the management to make it possible for people to recognize and develop these characteristics. The essential task of management is to arrange organizational conditions and methods of operation so that people can achieve their goals by directing their own efforts towards organizational objectives.

But Mc. Gregor says that though its application would be slow, it would bring about progress in both personal performance and improvement in the effectiveness of industrial organizations. Participative management and management by objectives are two modern methods of management which to large extent are based on Mc. Gregor's theory.

Clayton Alderfer's 'ERG' theory

Alderfer of Yale University has reworked Maslow's hierarchy of needs. Alderfer identified three groups of core needs.

1. Existence needs - E
2. Relatedness needs - R
3. Growth needs. - G

The existence needs are concerned with survival needs, (i.e., physiological and safety needs of Maslow)

The relatedness needs stress the importance of interpersonal, social relationship. (i.e., love need and esteem of Maslow)

According to Alderfer, more than one need may be operative at the same time and if a higher level need is not satisfied; the desire to satisfy a lower-level need increases.

Maslow said that there is a hierarchy (a step by step increase) of needs and only if the lower level need is satisfied, the higher level need satisfaction occurs. But Alderfer said that all the three-need categories work at the same time. He further says that a person who cannot achieve a higher need, or when he is frustrated, comes back to achieve a lower need.

Process theories

Process theories are concerned with the cognitive elements that go into motivation.

Victor H. Vroom's expectancy model

Vroom explained that a person's motivation towards and action at a particular time is determined by the anticipated value of all the outcomes (positive and negative) of the action, multiplied by the strength of a person's expectation that the action will lead to the outcome sought. In other words, motivation is the product of the anticipated values from an action and the perceived probability that these values will be achieved by the action. The anticipated value is called the "valance" and it is defined as the strength of a person's preference for one outcome in relation to others. The perceived probability is called "expectance" and it is defined as the strength of belief that a particular act will be followed by a particular outcome. Motivation is defined as the strength of drive towards action.

The motivational relationship is expressed in the formula

Valence x expectancy = motivation

Valence X expectancy
↓
Motivation
↓
Action
↓
Goal achievement
↓
Satisfaction

In order motivate a person to work we can do only two things. First, we can increase the positive value of the outcomes through such means as better communication about the outcomes' vales and actually increasing them. (i.e., increasing rewards). Second, we can increase his expectancy that the work will really lead him to the desired outcome; that is, we strengthen the connection between the work and the outcome. We can also do this by improved communications or we may increase the actual probabilities of the outcome.

Vroom's model is only a broad treatment of motivation, as it does not consider the individual's personality.

Porter-Lawler model of motivation

The various elements of this model are

a. Effort

If refers to the amount of energy extended by an employer on a given task. Perceived reward probability refers to the individual's perception of the probability that differential rewards depend upon differential amounts of effort. These two factors-values for reward and perception of effort-reward probability-determine the amount of effort that the employee will put it.

b. Performance

Effort leads to performance but both of these may not be equal; rather, performance is determined by the amount of effort and the ability and role perception of the individual. Thus if an individual has little ability and or inaccurate role perceptions, his performance may be ineffective in spite of his putting great efforts

c. Rewards

Performance is seen as leading to intrinsic rewards (such as a sense of accomplishment and actualization) and extrinsic rewards (such as working conditions and status). However, the intrinsic rewards are much more likely to produce attitudes about satisfaction that are related to performance. In addition, the perceived equitable rewards vitally affect the performance-satisfaction relationship. They reflect the fair level of rewards that the individual feels should be given for a given level of performance.

d. Satisfaction

Satisfaction is derived from the extent to which actual rewards fall short, meet or exceed the individual's perceived level of equitable rewards. In actual rewards meet or exceed perceived equitable rewards, the individual will feel satisfied. If these are less than equitable rewards, he will be dissatisfied. Thus this provides two implications. First, satisfaction is only in part determined by actual rewinds. Second, satisfaction is more dependent on performance than performance is on satisfaction. Only through the less direct feedback loops will satisfaction affect performance. This is a marked departure from the traditional analysis of the satisfaction-performance relationship.

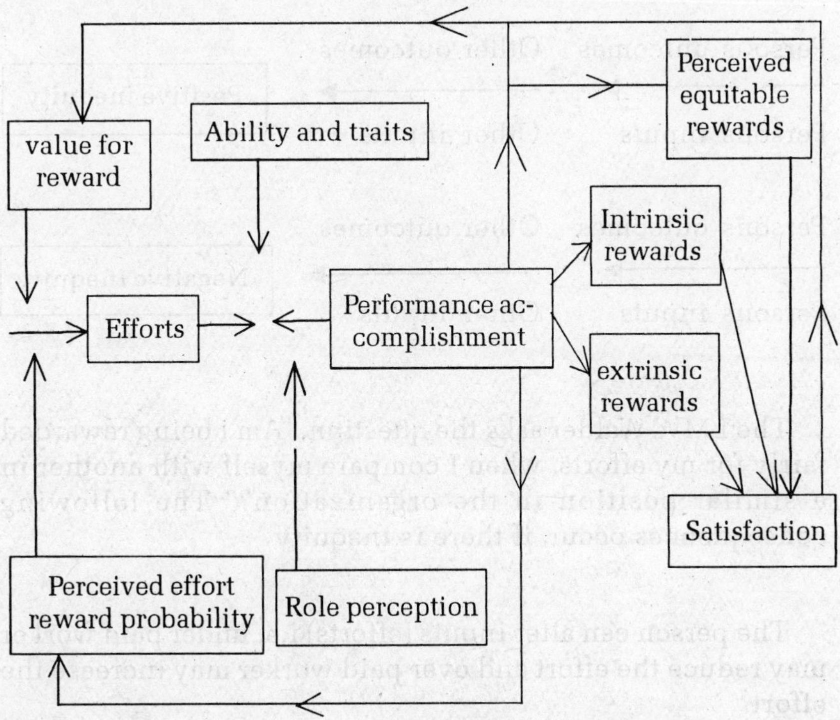

Importance of Porter-Lawler model

The manager matches the abilities of the individual to the requirement of the job.Explains the roles of employees. Explains the expected level of performance to the employees. Makes sure that the employee values the rewards.

Equity theory

Stacy Adams propounded the equity theory. Inequity, in simple terms is the injustice perceived by a person when he compares his outcomes his (rewards) to his inputs (effort), with the ratio of another person's outcomes to input and finds that they are not equal. A person working Lakshmi Machine Tool compares his counterpart at Praga Machine Tool, both situated at Coimbatore. If he perceives that his rewards, inputs ratio as higher than that of his counterpart, then it is known as positive inequity,

Persons outcomes / Persons inputs → Other outcomes / Other inputs → **Positive inequity**

Persons outcomes / Persons inputs → Other outcomes / Other inputs → **Negative inequity**

The LMW Welder asks the question, "Am I being rewarded fairly for my efforts, when I compare myself with another in a similar position in the organization?" The following consequences occur, if there is inequity

The person can alter inputs (efforts) i.e. under paid worker may reduce the effort and over paid worker may increase the effort.

The person might try to change the rewards of his company through 'unions' or individually. Sometimes the person might quit the job.

The person may try to reduce the inputs of the other person. He might altogether change the level of comparisons.

Managers of organization should be sensitive to such inequities perceived by the subordinates. When the subordinates visibly or openly react and show their dissatisfaction, managers might think of promotions or pay increases. At the same time, managers must give a continuous feedback on the appraisal of the subordinates. Felt inequities are common in organizations and hence it is important for managers to handle the situations.

17.7 Leadership

Definitions

Koontz and O'Donnell

"Leadership is the art of process of influencing people so that they will strive willingly towards the achievement of group goals".

Alten

"Leader is one who guides and directs other people. He must give effective direction and purpose".

Terry

"Leadership is the activity of influencing people to strive willingly for group objectives."

Keith Davis

"Leadership is the ability to persuade others to seek defined objectives enthusiastically."

Analysis of leadership

1. Leaders influence the behavior of others
2. Leadership is basically a personnel quality
3. There is relationship between leader and individuals
4. Leadership is a continuous process of influencing behavior
5. Leadership is exercised in a particular situation

Leaders use three different types of skills

1. Technical
2. Human and
3. Conceptual

1. Technical skills

Technical skills refer to a person's knowledge and ability in any type of process or technique. Examples are the skills learned by accountants, engineers, typists, and toolmakers.

2. Human skill

Human skill is the ability to think in terms of models, frameworks and relationship such as long range plans. It becomes increasingly important in higher managerial jobs.

3. Conceptual skill

It is the ability of the Leader to think in abstract, assess the environment and make decisions.

17.8 Essential qualities of a good leader

1. Intelligence

For effective leadership high level of intelligence is needed. Intelligence is a natural factor, which is directly proportional to development of brain. But intelligence can also be improved by the environment as well as by training. Although intelligence is a natural factor, research findings have proved that intelligence can be improved by means of effective training. Basic intelligence is required for keen observation, problem solving, logical reasoning, decision-making etc.

2. Emotional stability

A leader should be highly balanced, well adjusted and free from bias. A leader should be free from anger, should not have any anti-social attitude. In short, the leader should be frustration free.

3. Human relations

A successful leader should have adequate knowledge of human relations, i.e. how he should deal with human beings. Human relations are very vital for understanding and comprehending the members in order to get their voluntary co-operation. A good leader has intimate knowledge of the people and their relationships to each other.

4. Empathy

Empathy means understanding the things or the situations

from other man's point of view. A good leader should be more empathetic so that he knows, what the other fellow would think. A good leader should give respect to other persons, their rights, beliefs, values and feelings.

5. Technical skills

The leading of people requires the technical skills of managing people. Besides the skills, pertaining to the knowledge of the job, a leader should possess the qualities of managing people, like planning, organizing, coordination and controlling.

6. Motivating skills

Not only a leader is self-motivated but also he has the quality to motivate his followers. The leader can play a very vital role in stimulating the inner drives of his followers. So that they are highly motivated.

7. Communication skills

A leader for persuasive, informative and stimulating purposes should skillfully use communication. A good leader should communicate clearly, precisely and completely.

8. Decision making skills

Leadership is a process of decision-making. Quality, acceptance and effectiveness of the decision are three important needs. If the decision involves welfare of subordinates, leadership based on participation yields the highest level of quality and acceptance. If the leader can only make an effective decision, he should make it. Leader must involve himself in the decision making process in order to have effective decision and to protect against inferior decision.

Manager vs. Leader

S.No	Manager	Leader
1.	The manager administers, Carries out planning and budgeting	The leader innovates and charts a cause providing direction
2.	The management maintains	The leader develops Control and order.
3.	The manager is a copy	The leader is original
4.	The manager focuses systems, tasks, structures and results.	The leader focuses on people and process.
5.	The manager relies on control	The leader build relationship, inspires trust, motivates and generates commitment
6.	The manager has a short range view	Long-range perspective
7.	The manager asks how and why	The leader asks what and why
8.	The manager has his eye on the bottom line	The leader deals with the bottom line and has his eyes on the horizon
9.	The manager accepts and protects status quo	The leader is his own person and creates an environment for change.
10.	The manager does things right	The leader does the right things.

17.9 Theories of Leadership

Trait theory

Trait means 'characteristics'. And one can list a number of such qualities endlessly. In a study conducted on leadership, five qualities were considered to be the common qualities, like intelligence dominance, self-confidence, high-energy level and task-relevant knowledge.Keith Davis summarizes four of the major traits, which seem to have an impact on successful organizational leadership.

1. Intelligence

Research generally shows that the leader has higher intelligence than the average intelligence of his followers.

2. Social maturity and breadth

Leaders tend to be emotionally stable and mature and to have broad interests and activities.

3. Inner motivation and achievement drives

Leaders have relatively intense motivational drives of the achievement type. They strive for intrinsic rather than extrinsic rewards.

4. Human relations attitude

They always look at their subordinates from their point of view i.e. with empathy. They posses consideration and are employee – oriented rather than production-oriented.

Behavioral theories

Researchers were curious to find out how leaders behave?

For e.g. Are they democratic or autocratic? In the words of Stephen P. Robbins, "The difference between trait and behavioral theories, in terms of application, lies in their underlying assumptions. If trait theories were valid, then leaders are basically born;. You either have it or you do not. On the other hand, if there were specific behaviors that identified leaders, then we could teach leadership-we could design programmes for implanting these behavioral styles.

a. 'lowa' leadership studies

Ronald Lippitt and Ralph K. White, under the guidance of Kurt Lewin at the University of 'IOWA' conducted this study.A group of boys preferred democratic leadership rather than autocratic or Laissez fair leadership style. Iowa studies were the first to analyze leadership from the standpoint of scientific methodology and he revealed that different styles of Leadership can produce complex reaction from the same or similar groups.

b. 'Ohio' state leadership studies

In 1945, the Bureau of Business Research at Ohio State University initiated a series of studies on leadership. A questionnaire was prepared and a number of members of Air force were interviewed. The questionnaire LBDQ (Leadership behavior description questionnaire) and the findings were quite amazing, i.e. the same two dimensions of leadership continually emerged; they were in 83.2% of the studies. They are

1. Consideration
2. Initiating structure

1. Consideration

A person, who considers employees with empathy, friendly, approachable, and who show concern his followers' comfort, well being status and satisfaction.

2. Initiating structure

It is the ability of a leader to define and structure his or her role and those of the sub-ordinates the purpose of goal attainment. He defines patterns of organization, channels of communication, and ways of getting jobs done. It emphasizes the importance of task direction.

3. 'Michigan' studies

In 1947, the office of the Naval research requested the University of Michigan Survey Research Centre to study the principles, which contribute directly to productivity at the home office of the Prudential Insurance Company in Newyard, New Jersey. The Michigan group came up with two dimensions of leadership behavior

1. Employee oriented behavior
2. Production oriented behavior

1. Leaders of this type, emphasized interpersonal relations, took personal interest in their sub-ordinates and accepted individual differences among members.
2. Leaders of this type emphasized technical or task aspects of the job and their main concern was in accomplishing their group tasks and the group members were only the means of achieving end results.
3. Hersey – Blanchard's situational theory an important dimension that is neglected in most leadership theories, is that of the Maturity – dimension" of the followers. Paul Hersey and Ken Blanchard advocate that the leadership style must be suitability modified according to the maturity level of workers. Maturity may be classified as job-maturity and Psychological maturity. The first reveals ones knowledge and skills.

Psychological maturity relates to willingness or motivation to do something.

According to this theory two dimensions are used

a. Relationship behavior

b. Task behavior

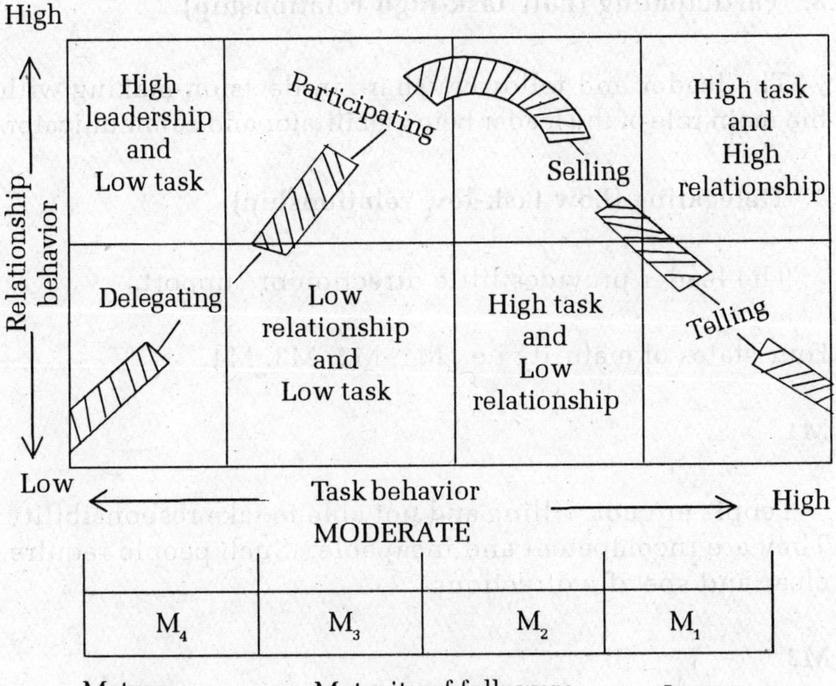

Hersey and Blanchard suggest 4 leadership styles. : Telling, Selling, Participating and delegating.

Leadership styles

1. Telling (High task low relationship)

The leader defines roles and tells people what, how when,

and where to do various tasks. It emphasizes directive behavior.

2. Selling (High task-high relatio.nship)

The leader provides both directive behavior and supportive behavior.

3. Participating (Low task-high relationship)

The leader and followers share in decision-making with the main role of the leader being facilitator and communicator.

4. Delegating (Low task-low relationship)

The leader provides little direction or support.

Four states of maturity i.e., M1, M2, M3, M4.

M1

People are not willing and not able to take responsibility. They are incompetent and incapable. Such people require, clear and specific directions.

M2

People are unable but willing to do necessary job tasks. They are motivated but currently lack the appropriate skills. Such people require high task and high relationship behavior.

M3

People are not willing to do what the leader wants and of course they are capable of doing jobs. Here the nest style required is participating style i.e., low task and high relationship style.

M4

People are both able and willing to do what is asked of them. Here only low task and low relationship style is required.

4. Fielder's contingency model of leadership

Research techniques: ASO and LPC

ASO means assumed similarity between opposites and LPC means least preferred co-workers. ASO calculates the degree of similarity between traders' perceptions of their most and least preferred co-workers.

LPC measures the degree to which leaders favorably perceive their co-workers.

A questionnaire was given to a number of leaders and their personality and leadership styles were identified. The leaders were classified into two types.

Type 1 Leader: Human relations expert

This leader does not tell many differences between the best worker and least preferred co-worker, because he treats all individuals very well and has high values on them. The leader gives even the least liked co-worker favorable description.

Type 2 Leader: Task directed style

This leader gives many differences between the best work and least preferred co-worker. He gives unfavorable description of the least preferred co-worker.

Contingency model

Fielder brings two aspects together i.e. Leadership style and the situational factors.

Leadership ----→	Situational
Styles ----→	Factors

According to fielder, the situation has three dimensions

1. The leader-member relations

If the relationship is good there is a favorable situation and if it is bad, then it is unfavorable situation.

2. Task-structure

If every job is clearly written with specifications then there is a favorable situation and if there are no clear procedures, it is unstructured, and the situation is unfavorable.

3. Position power

If the leader has powers to dismiss, appoint, promote or increase the salaries, then it is called favorable situation and if he has no powers, then it is clearly an unfavorable situation to the leaders.

Favorable situation means, all the above three dimensions are HIGH.

Unfavorable situation means, all the above three dimensions are LOW.

Findings

A good leader should use a particular leadership style in a specific situation for 'effectiveness'.

1. during very unfavorable and very favorable situations, the Task-directed leader was most effective.

2. during moderately favorable and moderately unfavorable situations, the human relations expert leader was more effective.

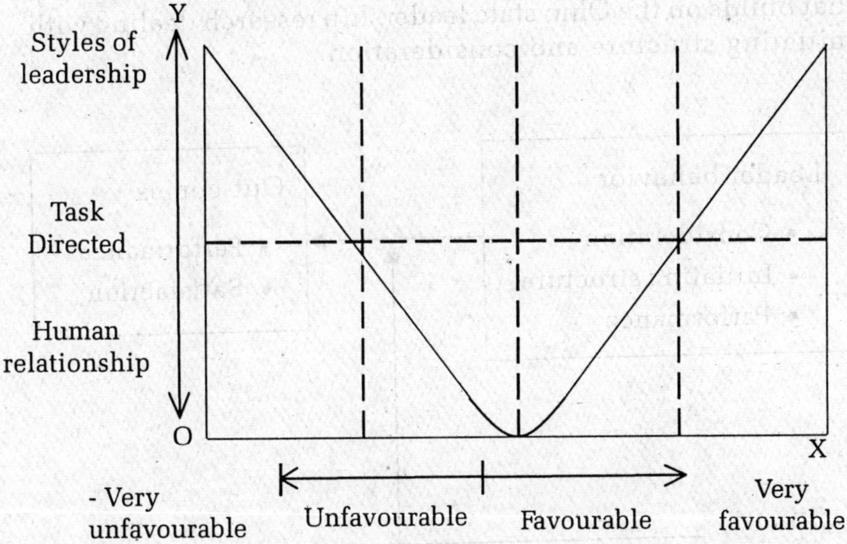

Favorableness of the situation

Why task directed leadership is successful in very favorable situations?

In very favorable conditions, where the leader has power, informal backing, and a relatively well-structured task, the group is ready to be directed, and the group expects to be told what to do. Ex. The Captain of an Airliner and his crew.

Why task directed Leadership is successful in very unfavorable situations?

If the dislike chairman of a committee asks for opinion and ideas on planning for a picnic on a Sunday, they would definitely say "we would like to go home". Here only task directed style is required.

5 Path-Goal theory

The path-goal theory is a contingency model of leadership that builds on the Ohio state leadership research dealing with initiating structure and consideration.

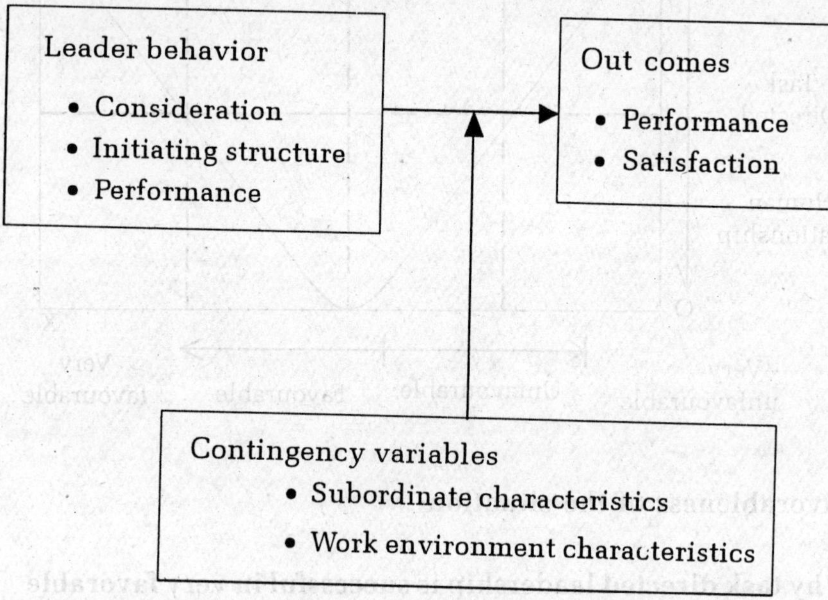

Leaders clarify the path to help their followers get from where they are to the achievement of their goals and make their journey along the path easier by reducing roadblocks and pitfalls. According to path-goal theory, a leader's behavior is acceptable to subordinates to the degree that it is viewed by them as immediate source of satisfaction or as a means of future satisfaction.

1. Makes subordinates need satisfaction contingent on effective performance and 2. provides the coaching, guidance, support and rewards that are necessary for effective performance.

Predictions of path-goal theory

It proposes that consideration is most helpful to subordinates in structured situations and less helpful in unstructured ones. Initiating structure will lead to greater satisfaction when the tasks are ambiguous or stressful than when they are highly structured and well laid out.

Where the tasks to be done are not clear, subordinate appreciate the leader clarifying the path to goal achievement. High consideration, on the other hand, results in high employee satisfaction when subordinates are performing structured or routine tasks. In clearly defined and structured tasks, efforts by the leader to explain tasks that are already clear will be seen by the subordinates as redundant or even insulting.

Leadership styles

'Style', Style means, the way in which the leader influences followers.

1 Robert R. Blake and Jane S. Mounton's leadership grid

Grid has two dimensions-concerns for people and concern for production. Concern for production is composed of the attitudes of a supervisor toward a wide variety of things such as creativeness of research, quality of staff service, work efficient and volume of output concern for people includes such things as degree of personal commitment towards goal achievement, maintenance of self of workers, provisions of good working conditions etc.

Managerial grid - phke and moltor

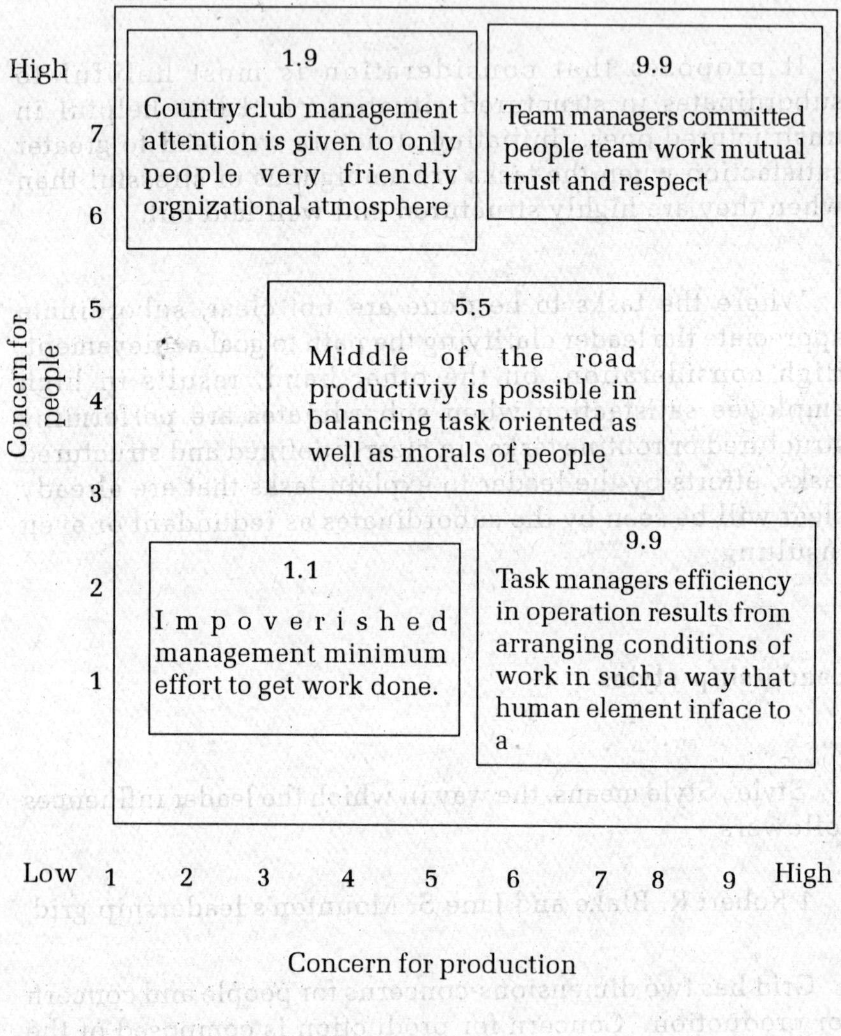

1.1

Under 1.1. Style of management, impoverished management managers concern themselves very little with either people or production and have minimum involvement in their jobs; for all purposes they just act as messengers communicating information from superiors to subordinates.

9.9

On the other hand, the 9.9 Managers display in their actions the highest possible dedication both to people and to production. They are the real 'team managers' who combine the production needs of the company with the needs of the individuals.

1.9

Country club management: Managers have little or no concern for production but are concerned only for people. No one is worried about company's objectives and the atmosphere is friendly, happy and relaxed.

9.1

The managers are called autocratic task managers who are concerned only with developing and efficient operation who have little or no concern for people and who are autocratic in their style of leadership.

5.5

Managers have medium concern for people and production. They do not set goals too high, and have rather benevolent autocratic styles of leadership.

The managerial grid is a useful device for identifying and classifying management styles. But it does not tell, why a manager fails in one part or another of the grid.

2. Reddin's three dimensional model

Blake and Mouton's grid identifies the style of a manager but does not directly relate to its effectiveness. William J.

Reddin, a Canadian professor and consultant, has added a third dimension to the model called "Effectiveness".

The center grid in this figure represents the four basic leadership styles. Reddin says that each of the four styles can be effective or ineffective, depending upon the situation.

The four styles on the upper right are effective and the four styles on the lower left are ineffective

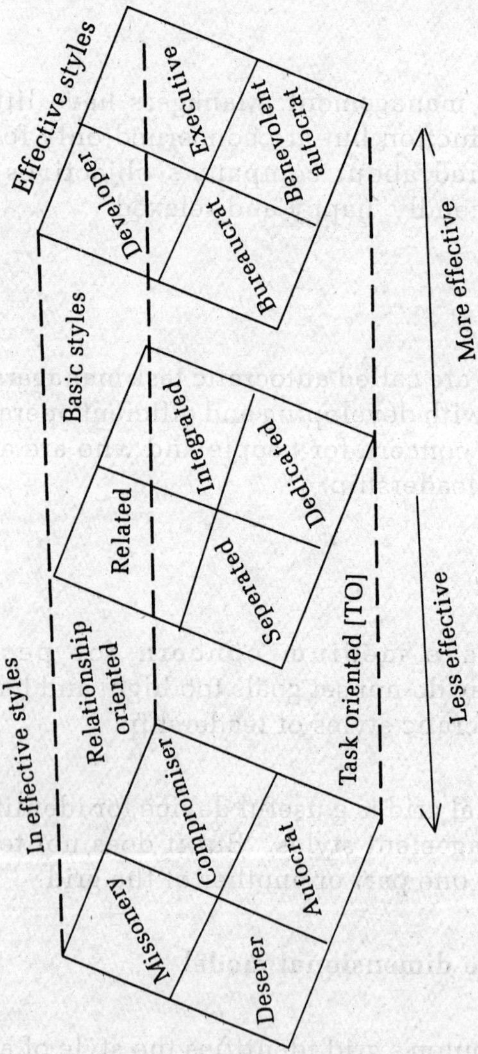

Briefly these eight styles are as follows

Effective styles

1. Executive

This style gives a great deal of concern to both (TO) task oriented and relationship oriented (RO). A manager is a good motivator, sets high standards, recognizes individual differences, and utilizes team management.

2. Developer

This style gives maximum concern to (RO) relationship and minimum concern to task (TO). He just develops people as individuals.

3. Benevolent autocrat

He gives maximum concern to task (TO) and minimum concern for relationship (RO). He knows exactly what he wants and how to get it without resentment.

4. Bureaucrat

He gives maximum concern to both (TO) and relationship (RO). He is interested in the rules and wants to maintain and control the situation by their use.

Ineffective styles

1. Compromiser

This style gives a great deal of concern for both task and relationship (TO & RO) in a situation that requires only emphasis on one or another. This style of manager is a poor decision-maker; the pressures affect him often too much.

		SYSTEM1	SYSTEM2	SYSTEM3	SYSTEM
	Leadership variables	Exploitative Autocratic	Benevolent Autocratic	Participative	Democratic
1	Confidence and Trust in Subordinate	Has no confidence and trust in subordinates	Has condescending confidence and trust	Substantial, but not complete confidence and trust : still wishes to keep control of the decisions	Complete confidence and trust in all matters
2	Subordinate's feeling of freedom.	Subordinates do not feel free at all to discuss things about the job with their supervisor.	Subordinates do not feel very free to discuss things about the job with their superiors.	Subordinates feel rather free to discuss things about the job with their superior.	Subordinates feel completely free to discuss things about the job with their superior.
3	Superior seeking involvement with their subordinates.	Seldom gets ideas and opinion of subordinates in solving job problems.	Sometimes gets ideas and opinions of subordinates in solving job problems.	Usually gets ideas and opinions and usually tries to make constructive use of them.	Always asks subordinates for ideas and opinions. Always tries to make constructive use of them

2. Missionary

This style gives maximum concern to people and relationships (RO) and minimum concern to the task (TO) where such behavior is inappropriate. This manager has no confidence in others and interested only in the immediate jobs.

3. Autocrat

This style gives maximum concern to the task (TO) and minimum concern for relationship (RO) where such behavior is inappropriate. This manager has no confidence in others and interested only in the immediate job.

4. Deserter

This style gives minimum concern to task (TO) and relationship (RO) in the situation where such behavior is inappropriate. This manager is uninvolved and passive.

Reddin's 3D approach emphasized that manager can be effective or ineffective depending up on the situation.

Leadership styles in a nutshell

1 Autocratic leadership

Features

1. A Manager centralizes Power in himself
2. He structures the complete work situation for his employees.
3. He wants all his employees to listen to him
4. Here the leadership is negative as the followers are uniformed, increase, and afraid of leader's authority.

2. Categories of Autocratic leadership

1. Strict autocratic leadership
2. Benevolent autocratic leadership
3. Incompetent autocratic leadership

1. Strict autocratic leadership

He follows autocratic styles in a very strict sense. He exercises negative motivation by imposing penalty.

2. Benevolent autocratic leadership

He also centralizes decision-making power in him but his motivation style is positive. He can be effective in getting efficiency in many situations, some people like to work under strong authority structure and they derive satisfaction by his leadership.

3. Incompetent autocratic leadership

Sometimes superiors adopt autocratic leadership style just to hide there in competency, because in other styles they may be exposed before their subordinates. However this cannot be used for a long time.

Advantages of Autocratic leadership styles

1. There are many subordinates in organization who prefer to work under centralized authority structure and strict discipline. They get satisfaction from this style.

2. It provides a strong motivation and reward to a manager exercising these styles.

3. It permits very quick decisions as a single person takes them.

4. Less competent subordinates also have scope to work in the organization under this leadership style as they do negligible planning, organization and decision-making.

Disadvantages

1. The people in the organization dislike it specially when it is strict and motivational style is negative.

2. Employees lack motivation. Frustration, low morale and conflicts develop in the organization decreasing the organizational efficiency.

2 Participative leadership style

Features

1. It is also called as democratic, consultative or ideographic.

2. Participation is mental and emotional involvement of a person in a group situation, which encourages him to contribute to group goals.

3. A manager decentralizes his decision-making process instead of taking unilateral decision.

4. He emphasizes consultation and participation.

5. The decisions are made on the basis of the suggestions and ideas of the subordinates. Finally, the superior gives credit to his-subordinates.

Merits

1. It is a highly motivating technique because the employees feel elated as their ideas and suggestions are given weightage in decision-making.

2. The Productivity is high.

3. The subordinates share the responsibility with superior and try to safeguard him also. It is said that the fellow in the boat never tries to make a hole.

4. The subordinates gain confidence as they grow up on the ladder of growth.

Demerits

1. Complex nature of organization requires a thorough understanding of its problem which lower level employees may not be able to do so. As such, participation does not remain meaningful.

2. Some people in the organization want minimum interaction with their superiors. For them participation technique is highly dangerous.

3. Participation is sometimes misused by employers. Employees prefer only autocratic leadership.

3 Free–Rein leadership

Features

1. This type of leadership gives complete freedom to subordinates.

2. In this style, manager once determines the policy, programmes and entire process of achievement of action is left with subordinates.

3. Group members perform everything and the manager usually contacts outside persons to bring the information to match with the group needs.

Advantages

1. This helps the subordinates to develop independent personality.

2. It is useful only in very few situations.

Limitations

1. The contribution of the manager is nil.

2. Generally productivity is low.

3. Individual freedom to the subordinates makes them relaxed towards organizations goals.

Review Questions

Two mark questions

1. Define Motivation?

2. Discuss the importance of Motivation?

3. Explain any three types of Motivation with an example?

4. What is ERG stands for?

5. Define Leadership?

6. "Is Leader the same as manager" Discuss?

Part - B

1. "Leaders are not born but made" comment?

2. Leadership is situational-Discuss?

3. What is Managerial Grid? How does a manager select his style according to this grid?

4. What is Three-dimensional Grid? What are the successful styles according to this?

5. Discuss the Path goal theory of Leadership?

6. Explain fully the concept of Hierarchy of needs?

7. Explain the Herzberg's theory of motivation?

8. Discuss the major assumptions of Theory X and Theory Y?

9. Explain Vroom's expectancy theory of motivation? How it is different from Porter lawler's approach?

Chapter - 18

Communication

18.1 Definitions

Newman

"Communication is an exchange of facts, ideas, and opinions by two or more persons".

M.Cunning

"Communication is the process of conveying messages (facts, ideas, attitudes and opinion) from one person to another, so that they are understood".

Keith Davis

"The process of passing information and understanding from one person to another".

Meaning

The term communication is derived from the Latin word "Communis", which means common communication means to inform, to tell, to show or to spread information. It is a process through which an information, idea or opinion is transferred to more number of persons.

18.2 COMMUNICATION PROCESS

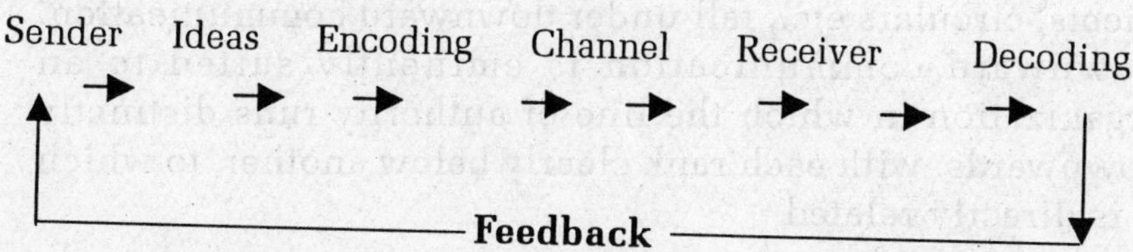

Sender – The person who intends to make contact with the objective of passing information, ideas to other persons is known as the sender.

Ideas – This is the subject – matter of communication. This might be opinions, attitudes, feelings, news, suggestions, orders & etc.

Encoding – The subject matter of communication is abstract and intangible, its transmission requires the use of certain symbols such as words, actions, pictures etc. Conversation of the subject matter into these symbols is the process of encoding.

Channel – These symbols are transmitted through certain channels e.g. radio/ telephone, air, etc., depending upon the situation of the two parties, viz., sender & receiver.

Receiver – Receiver is the person to whom the message is meant for.

Decoding – Receiver converts the symbol received from the sender to give him the meaning of the message.

Feedback – Feedback is necessary to ensure that the receiver has received the message and understands it in the some sense, as sender wants. Further, it also acts as an energizing factor, thereby changing the cause of action in the communication.

18.3 Downward communication

This communication flows from a superior to subordinate. Orders, individual instructions, Policy statements, job sheets, circulars etc., fall under downward communication. Downward communication is eminently suited to an organization in which the line of authority runs distinctly downwards, with each rank clearly below another, to which it is directly related.

Main objectives of downward communication

1. To gain specific directives about the job being entrusted to a subordinate. The decisions taken at the managerial level are transmitted to the subordinates staff in the form of directives so that the action may be initiated.

2. To explain policies and organizational procedures. A clear understanding of the policies gives the lower staff a wider perspective so that they can grasp and play their role more meaningfully.

3. To appraise the subordinates of their performance. If the performance of a subordinate is objectively assessed and the assessment communicated to him in a considerate tone, it will definitely promote his efficiency.

4. To give information about the rationale of the job, i.e., to explain to a subordinate the significance of the job assigned to him and why he has been entrusted with it.

Limitations of downward communication

Under–communication and over–communication

Either under– communication or over-communication often carries downward communication. i.e., a superior may either talk too little or too much about a job.

Delay

The lines of communication in downward communication being very long, transmitting information to the lowest worker is a time-consuming process. By the time information reaches him, it may have lost much of its significance, or it may have caused damaging delay.

Loss of information

Unless the communication is fully written, it is not likely to be transmitted downwards fully. A part of it is almost certain to be lost. In fact, it has been experimentally verified that only 20 per cent of the communication sent downward through five levels of management finally gets to the worker's level.

Distortion

In long lines of communication, information is not only lost but also even distorted.

Built in resistance

The subordinates do not get any opportunity of participating in the decision-making process. They are expected to receive the policy decisions and directives without questioning their appropriateness, utility or validly which they resent.

18.4 Upward communication

The communication channel, which pushes the flow of information upwards, is known as the upward channel of communication. Managers have only recently come to recognize the importance of upward communication.

Importance of upward communication

Providing feedback

Upward communication provides the management with necessary feedback.

Outlet for the pent-up emotion

Upward communication gives the employees an opportunity to vent their problems and grievances.

Constructive suggestions

Often employees offer constructive suggestions to promote the welfare of the organization. Some of these suggestions, when implemented, definitely prove beneficial.

Easier introduction of new schemes

Since employees feel themselves to be a party to the decision-making process, it helps the organization to introduce new schemes without unduly antagonizing the employees.

Organizational solidarity and cohesion

The existence of the grapevine proves that the workers are interested in their associates. The very fact that they talk among themselves helps to promote organizational solidarity and cohesion.

Supplement to other channel

All information cannot be transmitted to the employees through the official channels. If there is some useful information unsuitable for being transmitted through official channels, it can be transmitted through the grapevine.

Quick transmission

The speed with which information is transmitted through the grapevine is just remarkable.

Feedback

The grapevine provides feedback to the management.

18.5 How to use grapevine effectively?

1. The managers should try to spot the leaders. They should try to find out the people who are more active

on the grapevine and keep them well informed, so that harmful rumors do not reach the employees.

2. The grapevine should be used to feel the pulse of the employees.

3. If there is any false rumor, the management should immediately use the official channels to contradict and to dispel the fears of the employees.

4. If the workers are associated with decision-making, the rumormongers will be automatically frustrated. If the workers are already aware that the plant is to be modernized but that the modernization process is not going to involve any retrenchments, the arrival of the new machinery and engineers will not cause any undue apprehensions among them. Thus the harmful effects of the grapevine will be successfully counteracted.

Consensus

In the commercial field, it is felt desirable that when the board meeting is held, decision should be arrived at through consensus. Unanimous decisions help to project a good image of the organization among the employees as well as shareholders.

18.6 Communication media

The subject matter of communication, i.e., message, ideas, suggestions etc., being abstract and intangible, their transmission and receipt require use of certain symbols, which become the media of communication. These symbols may be (i) word either oral or written, (ii) pictures including graphs and diagrams; and (iii) actions or gestures including facial expressions. Each of these media may be either used exclusively, that is, to the complete exclusion of others, or, as is very commonly the case, two or more of these may be used to supplement each other. For example, in face-to-face communication, diagrams and charts may be used to clarify what one is talking about. Of these, oral and written methods of communication are the most important.

Barriers in communication

There might be a number of such barriers impeding the flow of communication in the organization. These may be classified as (i) Semantic (ii) Emotional or psychological barriers (iii) Organizational and (iv) Personal factors.

Semantic barriers are obstruction caused in the process receiving or understanding of the message during the process of encoding and decoding ideas and words. These barriers arise from the linguistic capacity of the parties involved. The following are some semantic barriers.

Badly expressed message

Lack of clarity and precision in a message makes it badly expressed. Poorly chosen and empty words and phrases, careless omission, lack of coherence, bad organization of ideas, awkward sentence structure, inadequate vocabulary, platitudes, numbing repetition, jargon, and failure to clarify implication are some common faults in this case.

Faulty translations

Every manager receives various types of communication from superiors, peers, subordinates and he must translate information destined for subordinates, peers and superiors into language suitable to each. Hence the message has to be put into words appropriate to the frame work in which the receiver operates.

Unclarified assumptions

There are certain uncommunicated assumptions, which underline practically all messages. Though a message appears to be specific its underlying assumptions may not be clear to the receiver.

Specialists language

It is often found that technical personnel and special groups tend to develop a special, peculiar, and technical language of their own. This increases their isolation from others and builds a communication barrier.

Emotional or psychological barriers

Premature evaluation

Rogers and Roethlisberger in 1952 first pointed out this barrier. Evaluation is the tendency of prematurely evaluating communications, rather than to keep uncompromised position during the interchange. This barrier can be remedied by "empathy" and non-evaluative listening.

Inattention

The preoccupied mind of a receiver and the result non-listening is one of the major chronic psychological barriers. It is a common phenomenon that people simply fail to react to bulletins, notices, minutes and reports.

Loss by transmission and poor retention

When communication passes through various levels in the organization, successive transmission of the same message are decreasingly accurate. It is said that, in case of oral communication about 30% of the information is lost in each transmission.

Distrust of communication

It arises out of ill- considered judgment or illogical decisions or frequent countermanding of the original communication by the communicator. Repeated experience of this kind gradually conditions the receiver to delay action or act unenthusiastically hence making the communication unsuccessful, though apparently it is complete.

Failure to communicate

It is quite an accepted fact that managers often fail to transmit the needed messages. This might be because of laziness on the part of the communicator, or assuming that "everybody knows". Or procrastination or "hogging" information or deliberately to embarrass others.

Organizational barriers

Organizational policy

The general organizational policy regarding communication act as an overall guideline to everyone in the organization regarding how he is normally expected to behave in this matter.

Organizational rules and regulations

Organizational rules and regulations affect the flow of communication by prescribing the subject matter to be communicated and also the manner through which these are to be communicated. The rules may restrict the flow of certain messages and may leave many important ones. On the other hand, communication through proper channel in a specified way prescribed by these rules delays it and works against the willingness of persons to convey the message. This barrier is strongly operative in Indian Public Sector enterprises where observance of rules and regulations are more rigid.

Status relationships

The placing of people in superior subordinate capacity in

the formal organization structure also blocks the flow of communication and more particularly in upward direction. Greater the difference between hierarchical positions in terms of their status, greater would be the possibility of communication breakdown.

Complexity in organization structure

In an organization where there are a number of managerial levels, communication gets delayed. Chances of communication getting distorted are more in case of upward communication, because people generally do not like to pass up the adverse or criticism either of themselves or of their superiors.

Organizational facilities

Organizational facilities provided for smooth, adequate, clear and timely flow of communication might take a number of forms. Some of these have been mentioned earlier in the communication media such as meetings, conferences, complaint box, suggestion box, open door system, social and cultural gatherings etc. If these are not properly emphasized generally people fail to make effective communication.

Personal barriers

A plethora of factors internal to the two parties-sender and receiver-to this process also exert important influences on its operation, as communication is basically an Inter-personal process.

Barriers in superiors

Attitude of superiors

The attitudes of superiors towards communication in general or in any particular direction affect the flow of message in different directions. For example, if this attitude is unfavorable, there is greater possibility that messages would not flow adequately from and or to superiors.

Fear of challenge to authority

A person in the organization always tries to get higher positions and prestige to satisfy his needs. As such managers in general try to withhold the information coming down the line or going up as frequent passing or information may disclose their weakness.

Insistence on proper channel

Once of the features of superior's exercising of the authority is that they wish to remain in communication links and they do not like any type of bye – passing in communication.

Lack of confidence in subordinates

Superiors generally perceive that their subordinates are less competent and capable, they are not able to advise superiors or they may not have some information coming downwards.

Ignoring communication

Sometimes superiors consciously and deliberately ignore the communication from their subordinates to maintain their importance.

Lack of time

Superiors feel, whether correct or otherwise, that they are overburdened with the work and they have little time to talk about their policy matters.

Lack of awareness

Sometimes superiors may lack awareness about the

significance and usefulness of communication in directions in general or of a particular subject – matter. In such a case, communication flow is blocked.

Barriers in subordinates

Vertical communication in either direction can take place only when subordinates also actively participate in this process. There are various factors in the subordinates that adversely affect such active participation on their part. Some factors, which have been traced in the case of superiors, are also applicable here, such as attitude, time availability, awareness about the significance, etc.

Lack of proper incentive

Lack of motivation to communicate also prevents subordinates to communicate upwards. The reward and punishment system of the organization is more responsible for this. If a novel suggestion by a subordinate does not evoke any attention from the organization, he would not convey it.

18.7 How to make communication effective?

There are various guidelines for making effective communication. American Management Association has suggested Ten Commandments of good communication.

Clarity in idea

The communicator should be quite clear about what he wants to communicate. Communication is a process starting with ideation, which includes generation of ideas, which are meant for communication. This is the subject matter of communications and may include opinions, attitudes, feelings, views, suggestions, orders etc.

Purpose of communication

Every communication has some purpose, the basic purpose, of any communication being to get behavioral response from the receiver of the communication. However the ultimate objective may be extended further, for example, getting an order accepted by the subordinate. The communication should be directed towards this objective by the efforts of communicator.

Empathy in communication

The way for effective communication is to be sensitive towards receiver's needs, feelings, and perceptions. This is what psychologist call empathy in communication, implying putting laze in other's shoes.

Two-way communication

Communication is a two-way traffic and this fact must be realized in communication. Two-way communication brings two minds together which is the basic core of any communication. It involves a continuous dialogue between sender and receiver of the message.

Appropriate language

Decoding it into some symbols transmits the subject matter of communication. Such symbols may be in the form of words, either spoken or written, and gestures. If words are used, the language used for communication should be such, which is understandable by the receiver.

Supporting words with action

Often it is said that action speaks louder than words. While communicating, the sender may use the actions to emphasize a point. This will ensure seriousness in communication.

Credibility in communication

One criterion for effective management communications is that it has demonstrated through his competence that he is worthy for trust. He must also maintain his trust and creditability. Subordinates will follow thus any communication, which is based on this trust and creditability.

Good listening

A communicator must be a good listener too. By this process, he is not only giving chance for others to speak but gathers useful information for further communication. By concentrating on the speaker's explicit and implicit meanings, the manager can obtain a much better understanding of what is being said. Nicholas has identified that managers suffer from some common habits of bad listening. Davis has suggested ten points, which may be observed in listening. These are: Stop talking, put the talker at ease, show the talker that you want to listen to, remove distractions, empathize with the talker, be patients, hold your temper, go easy on arguments and criticism, ask questions, stop talking. He has emphasized stop talking because without stopping talking, one cannot listen to.

Review Questions

Two mark questions

1. Define Communication?
2. Draw the diagram of Communication process?
3. What do you mean by Downward communication?
4. What do you mean by Upward communication?
5. What is Grapeview?

Part - B

1. What is communication? What are the types of communication?

2. "Communication is sharing of understanding" Discuss this and bring out the process of communication?

3. What are the various types of communication media? Discuss the relative merits and demerits of oral and written communication?

4. What are the essential characteristics of a good communication system? Discuss the steps for making communication effective?

5. What are the different barriers of communication? What steps can be taken to overcome these barriers?

Chapter - 19

Controlling

19.1 Introduction

Control is the last function of management. The controlling function will be unnecessary to the management if other functions of managements are performed properly. If there is any imperfection in the planning and actual performance, control will be needed. The deviations are set right by the controlling function. This function ensures desired results., Planning identified the activities and controlling regulates the activities. Success or failure of planning depends upon the result of success or failure of controlling.

Definitions

Earnest Dale

"Control envisages a system that not only provides a historical record of what has happened to the business as a whole, but, pinpoints the reasons why it has happened and provides data that enables the chief executive or the departmental head to take corrective steps if he finds that he is on the wrong track".

E.F.L. Brech

"Control – checking current performance against pre-determined standards contained in the plans, with a view to ensure adequate progress and satisfactory performance, also recording the experience gained from the working of these plans as a guide to possible operations."

Billy E. Goetz

"Management control seeks to compel events to form to plans".

Koontz and O'Donnell

" Controlling is the measurement of accomplishment against the standards and the correction of deviations to assure attainment of objectives according to plans".

Henry Fayol

"Control consists in verifying whether everything occurs in conformity, is with the plans adopted, the instructions issued and principles established. It has for its object to point out weaknesses and errors in order to rectify them and prevent recurrence."

George R. Terry

"Controlling is determining what is being accomplished, that is, evaluating the performance and if necessary, applying corrective measures so that the performance takes place according to plans."

Robert N. Anthony

"Management control is the process by which managers assure that resources are obtained and used effectively and efficiently in the accomplishment of an organization's objectives."

Mary Cusing Niles

"Control thus viewed, is an aspect and projection of planning whereas planning sets the course to the chosen courses or to an appropriately changed one."

Haynes and Massie

"Control is that function of the system which provides direction in performance to the plans."

Dalton E. Mc Farland

"The presence in a business of that force which guides it to a pre-determined objective by means or pre-determined objective by means of pre-determined policies and decisions."

Areas or Scope of Control

The term control covers all the activities of a business concern. The main area of control is as follows:

1. Control over the policies of the concern.
2. Control over organization.
3. Control over the personnel employed in an organization.
4. Control over capital available to the concern.
5. Control over capital expenditure.
6. Control over production.
7. Control over wages and salaries paid to the employees.
8. Control over the cost of production.
9. Control over public relations.
10. Control over research and development.

11. Control over tools and equipments.

12. Overall control

19.2 Steps in Control Process

Control points out the deviations of the plans and suggests remedial action to improve future plans. Some of the procedures are to be found defective because of human limitations. So, control is necessary and it has the following steps:

1. Establishing standards.

It is necessary to find the results which are desired. It is very useful to setting the standards. If it is not, useful control will not be possible. Standards may be quantitative or qualitative. Number of units produced, number of men, hours employed, total cost incurred, revenue earned, the amount of investments etc., are some of the examples of quantitative standard. If expression of standards in quantitative terms is not possible, they will be expressed in qualitative terms such as goodwill, employee's morals, motivation etc.

The standard should have some characteristics to produce effective performance. The characteristics may be time, cost, efforts, results oriented, quantitative terms expressed, accurate, periodical revision and the like.

2. Measuring performance.

The performance should be compared with the established standards. So, necessary information should be collected about the performance. The effective management information system provides the necessary information i.e., performance particulars. If standards are expressed in quantitative terms, quantitative information can be collected.

In other words, if standards are expressed in qualitative terms, qualitative information's can be collected. Several techniques are used by the management to measure the performance.

3. Comparison of actual with standards.

Whenever the actual performance is compared with standards, the management knows the deviations. Then, the management may find the extent of deviations and identify the reasons for deviations. Comparison is very easy when standards are expressed in terms of quantity. If results are intangible or qualitative, personnel observation will be used to find out the extent of deviation.

When the actual performances are equal to the standards, there is no need for further action. Control process comes to an end with this stage. However, if the standards are not achieved, the management has to decide the type of corrective action.

All the deviations need not be reported to the management. Deviations, which are beyond the reasonable limits, should be reported to the top management. This is termed as control by exception or management by exception. Then, the reasons and causes for the deviations are analyzed. The causes may be controllable or non-controllable. The management has to take necessary corrective action only in case the causes are controllable. However, no need will arise to the management to take corrective actions if the causes are uncontrollable.

4. Taking corrective action.

Management has to find the causes of deviation before taking corrective action. The causes of deviation may be due to ineffective and inadequate communication, defective system of wage payment, defective system of selection of personnel, lack of proper training, lack of motivation, ineffective supervisions and the like. The management has to take necessary corrective action on the basis of nature of causes of deviations.

19.3 Techniques of Control

The management for controlling the various deviations in the organization uses various methods. The nature and use of managerial control techniques are discussed below.

1. Statistical control reports

These types of reports are prepared and used in large organizations. Reports are prepared in quantitative terms. Then, the variations from standards are easily measured. In this way, the management exercises control. A periodical report of sales volume is an example of statistical control reports.

2. Personal observation

Using this technique, the manager personally observes the operations in the work place. The manager corrects the operations whenever the need arises. This is the oldest method of control. Employees work cautiously to get better performance. The reason is that their supervisor personally observes them. Personal observation is a time consuming technique and the supervisor does not have enough time to afford personal observation. The honest and efficient employee dislikes personal observation technique. The observer may be biased in performance evaluation.

3. Cost accounting and cost control

Profit of any business depends upon the cost incurred to run a business. Profit is maximized by reducing the cost of operation or production, so, the business concern gives much importance to the cost accounting and cost control. Management uses a number of systems for determining the cost of products and services. The cost accounting procedures and methods differ from one industry to another according to the nature of industry. They are used for effective cost control and cost reduction.

4. Break-even analysis

It is otherwise called as 'cost volume profit analyses. It analyses relationship among cost of production, volume of production, volume of sales and profits. Here, total costs are divided into two i.e., fixed cost and variable cost. Fixed cost will never change according to the changes in the volume of production. Variable cost varies according to the volume of production. This analysis helps in determining the volume of production or sales and the total cost which is equal to the revenue. The excess of revenue over total cost is termed as profit. The point at which sales is equal to the total cost is 'Break Even Point' (BEP). In other words, the break-even point is the point at which there is no profit or loss.

The break-even point is calculated with the help of the following formulae:

$$\text{BEP} = \frac{\text{Fixed Cost}}{\text{Selling price per unit} - \text{Variable price per unit}}$$

(Or)

$$\text{BEP} = \frac{\text{Fixed Cost}}{\text{Contribution per unit}}$$

Contribution per unit = Selling price per unit – Variable cost per unit.

The break-even point analysis helps to managerial control in several ways.

5. Special control reports

This report may or may not contain statistical data. Using this technique, a particular operation is investigated at a specified time for a particular purpose. This is done according to the requirements of management but not in regular basis. The deviations from standards are paid additional attention and corrective action is taken. Handling complaints of damage is an example of this type of control techniques.

6. Management audit

Management audit is an independent process. It aims at pointing out the inefficiency in the performance of management functions such as planning, organizing, staffing, directing, controlling and suggesting possible improvements. It helps the management to handle the operations in an effective manner. Management audit is not a compulsory and not enforced by law.

7. Standard costing

Standard costing is used to control the cost. The following are the steps involved in standard costing:

A. Determination of cost standards for various components such as material, labor and overhead.

B. Measurement of actual performance.

C. Comparison of actual cost with standard cost to find variations.

D. Finding the causes of variations.

E. Taking measures to avoid the variations in future.

8. Return on Investment

Return on investment is also known as return on the capital employed. Using this technique, the rate of profitability is identified by the management. The amount of profits earned by the company is different from the rate of profitability of the company. The difference between the cost and revenue is profit. The rate of profitability is the earning capacity of the company. Return on investments is calculated by dividing the net profit with the total investment or capital employed in the business organization.

9. Internal audit

Internal audit report is prepared at regular intervals, normally by months. It covers all the area of operations. This report is sent to the top management. The management takes steps to control the performance on the basis of the report. Internal audit report emphasis the degree of deviations from the expectations. It is very useful to attain the objectives on timely basis.

10. Responsibility accounting

The performance of various people is judged by assessing how far they have achieved pre-determined objectives. The objectives are framed section-wise, department-wise and division-wise and assessed similarly. Costs are allocated department-wise rather than product-wise. Each department, section or division, is fixed as responsible centers. An individual is responsible for his area of operation in a particular section, department or division.

11. Managerial Statistics

Using the managerial statistics technique, the manager compares the past results with current results in order to know the causes for changes. These are very useful to the management in planning and decision-making for the future. According to Kenton. Hauson, "Managerial statistics deal with the data and methods which are useful to management executives in planning and controlling of organization activities."

12. Performance evaluation and review technique (PERT)

This technique is used to solve the problem which crops up once or few times. It is not useful in tackling the problems which come up continuously. The PERT was developed by Bozo. Allen and Hamilton. They used this technique in Polaris Submarine Project under the sponsorship of U.S. Navy. The PERT technique is very useful for construction projects, publication of books etc.

13. Critical Path Method (CPM)

This technique also allows the principle of PERT. The technique concentrates on cost rather than duration. CPM assumes that duration of every activity is constant. Time estimate is made for each activity. CPM technique was developed by a group of employees of DU de Nemours Company.

14. Gantt Milestone Chart

This technique was a old one and at present, it is not in use. The reason is that this technique emphasizes only in production scheduling but not on product quality. This technique was pro-founded by Henry. I. Gantt.

15. Production Control

The production control technique is necessary for smooth functioning of an organization. Production control involves planning of production, determination of stock level of raw materials, finished goods, selection of process, selection of tools in production, etc. According to Spiegel, "Production control is the process of planning in advance of operations, establishing the exact route of each individual item, part of assembly and the finished product and releasing the necessary orders as well as initiating the required follow up to effectuate the smooth functioning of the enterprise."

16. Management Information System

Relevant information is collected and transferred to all the persons who are responsible to take decisions. A communication system is developed through which all levels of persons are informed about the growth of the organization. Whenever the deviation is found, the corrective or control action is taken by the responsible person. The management information system emphasizes the need for adequate information in time for taking the best decision. Thus, management information system helps the management in managerial decision-making by giving the right information at the right time and in the right form.

17. External Audit Control

External audit is a must to all the joint stock companies under the purview of statutory control. So, it is otherwise known as statutory and control. This type of audit protects the interests of the shareholders and creditors of the company. The external auditor certifies that all the books of accounts are kept as per the requirements of law and supplies all the necessary information for the purpose of audit and the balance sheet presents a true and fair view. The external audit is conducted by the qualified auditor. The qualifications of such type of auditor is fixed by the Central Government.

18. Zero-base budgeting

There is a new technique and has become popular within a short period. It is a new approach to budgeting.

Zero-base budget is prepared without considering the previous year's figures. This technique requires the recalculation of all organization activities to ascertain which should be eliminated or reduced or increased. In other words, the funds are estimated at current requirements. It means finding out how much amount is necessary to complete an ongoing project.

19. Standing orders

Standing order covers rules and regulations, discipline, procedure and the like. Rules and regulations are framed according to the requirements of administration. For example, no employee should leave the office before office time without getting prior permission in writing.

Review questions

Two mark questions

1. Define Controlling?
2. What is BEP?
3. What is ROI?
4. What is CPM?
5. Define zero base budgeting?

Part-B

1. What are the requirements of an Effective Control system?
2. Explain the Importance of Control in a Business Organization?
3. Discuss the Techniques involved in control?

Chapter - 20

International Management and the Future

20.1 International Management and the Future

The Empirical approach gave us a plethora of cases of practical experiences by which today we see a new concept emerging out "the strategic management". Similarly the systems approach has also been used by many organizations. For e.g., the managers of multi-national organizations have started viewing their operations as a global interdependent system. The situational or contingency approaches have stressed that whether it is Japan or France or India, management depends on the realities of the situation. The new managerially oriented organizational development has started viewing that basic management theory and techniques fit well into the programmes of behavioral interventions. McKinsey's 7'.S. Frame work highlights a model that is close to the operational or management process model. The 7'.S are 1) Strategy 2) Structure 3) Systems 4) Style 5) Staff 6) Shared values 7) Skills.

20.2 Increasing Internationalization of the World Economy

The economics of all nations have become interdependent. Companies and individuals can own foreign assets either by purchasing shares in other companies, which own the assets, or by going multinational and managing assets directly. Today many companies are going international and internationalization is dependent on the following factors.

a. Directness of the company's international involvement.

b. The Company's organizational structure.

c. The importance of the company's international concerns relative to its domestic ones.

Howard Pertimutter has identified three primary attitudes among the managers of International Companies: Ethnocentric, polycentric and geocentric. Ethnocentric managers see foreign countries and their people as inferior to those of the home country. A Polycentric manager see all countries as different and as hard to understand. This is based on the notion, it is best to give foreign subsidiaries, staffed by local nation, a great deal of managerial freedom. Geocentric managers accept both similarities and differences between domestic and foreign management policies and strike a balance between those that are most effective.

20.3 What is Multinational Corporation (MNC)?

MNC is an organization that is engaged in production or services through its own association in several countries, manages and controls the overall activities from a global perspective.

Multinational companies are large in size and are engaged in substantial amount of business throughout the world.

"A Multinational Enterprise is a cluster of corporation controlled by one head quarter but with operations spread over many countries" – Stephen H. Roebuck and Kenneth Simmonds.

Christopher Korth has identified the following to the MNCs.

Transfer of capital, technology and entrepreneurship to the host country.

Improvement of the host country's balance of payments.

Creation of local jobs and career opportunities.

Improved competition in the local economy.

Greater availability of products to the local consumers.

20.4 Strategies of Multinational Corporations

The environmental factors that affect domestic firms are more important for MNC's, in foreign countries. The managers must interact with people who have different educational and cultural backgrounds and value systems; managers must cope with legal, political and economical factors.

Strategies of MNC's are dependant on 'who' performs the management activity in the host country? Local or foreigners? If local people do the management, three types of strategies can be formulated. They are a) Import – Export b) Licensing c) Contracting with turn key projects. Import – Export strategy means that the foreign firm just merely purchases or sells products from an independent firm. Licensing strategy denotes that there is a licensing agreement for producing goods in the host country royalty payments. The strategy of contracting and turnkey projects would mean that often a host country firm or government will enter into a contract facility when a local firm doesn't possess the expertise (e.g. dam, railroad, airport etc.) The project is completed and turned over to the local people to operate (turnkey project). Sometimes a foreign firm may be asked to manage operations in a complex industry in which its employees do not have any expertise.

Strategies are to be modified suitably with the foreign investments also. If host country laws permit foreign investment or ownership of assets, their joint ventures are possible which means sharing ownership in its foreign subsidiaries with other foreigners or local interests. "When a multinational organization progresses to a position where it is no longer views its international operation as a collection of diverse foreign subsidiaries, but instead develops a strategy that attempts to maximize results from totality of the firm's operation. It has adopted a 'global strategy' (Roebuck and Simmons). To adopt a global strategy, top management must view the total market as a global market and a total source of inputs and then select a strategy designed to maximize the output from the world. The management practices in various countries and the recent trends in management are quite fascinating. For instance, the traditional style of German managers was authoritarian, but today they give way to participative approaches. According to recent labor law the German laborers are given opportunities to participate in the supervisory board and the executive committee. This principle is called co-determination principle.

In France, Government planning on a national scale helps to co-ordinate plans of individual industries and companies. There is a significant importance given to managerial function of planning. Today, the trend is that there is a close relationship between government planning and firms especially those that are owned and directly aided by government. In Australia managing is influenced by that country's moralistic stance and its emphasis is on political and social value, achievement and risk taking. Italians are highly competitive but at the same time like group decision making. In Britain, adaptability, individualism, resourcefulness and logic are highly valued. In USA, there is an upsurge of foreign managers from Japan, and other countries. In order to avoid the cultural shock to foreigners, the U.S. companies are now focusing on the ways and means of reducing the cultural shock in training.

20.5 Japanese Management and U.S. Management

The Japanese management practice includes two vital principles:

a. Life-time employment.

b. Consensus Decision-making.

The Japanese always gives importance to the individual employee, his seniority and his life long employment and this enhances employee loyalty. About one third of the Japanese labor force is well under the cover of job-security system. This practice of decision-making is built on the concept that change and new ideas come primarily from below. Since it is group decision-making the Japanese are slow in making decision, but fast in implementation. When a wrong decision is taken, the blame is shared by all. In the case of U.S. Management, decisions are taken at the top, the individual takes the decision and when the decision goes wrong, it becomes an affair of fixing blame on the individual superior.

Theory 'Z'

This theory emphasizes interpersonal skills needed for group interaction. Although decisions are taken in group, the responsibility lies with the individual. In U.S.A, many companies suffered from productivity crisis. As a result some companies started adopting the principles of Japanese management. For e.g.: participative management, the Japanese practice of infrequent performance evaluation, but promotions is not emphasized by Theory – Z type companies. In short, companies selectively use some Japanese managerial practices making adjustments according to the situations of the environment.

Review Questions

Two mark questions:

1. Define Globalization?

2. What is MNC?

Part-B

1. Discuss the trend towards Globalization of the theory of Management?

2. What are the Strategies of Multinational companies?

3. Discuss the various Trends of Management in Japan and USA?